The Picture History of the BOSTON BRUINS

THE PICTURE
BOSTON

HISTORY OF THE BRUINS

From Shore to Orr and the Years Between

by Harry Sinden and Dick Grace

THE BOBBS-MERRILL COMPANY, INC.
Indianapolis • New York

Published by the Bobbs-Merrill Company, Inc.
Indianapolis   New York

Designed by Viki Webb
Manufactured in the United States of America

First printing

U.S. LIBRARY OF CONGRESS CATALOGING IN PUBLICATION DATA

Sinden, H.

    The picture history of the Boston Bruins.

    1. Boston Bruins—History. I. Grace, Dick.
II. Title
GV848.B6G72   796.9[62]0974461   75–6398
ISBN 0–672–52159–8

The 1924 Bruins team picture. Front row: *Werner Schnarr, George Redding, Lloyd Cook, Carson Cooper, Bobby Rowe, Art Ross (Manager)*
Back row: *Hec Fowler, Jimmy Herberts, Archie Skinner, Smokey Harris, Curley Headley, Herb Mitchell, Tommy Murray (Trainer)*

THIS BOOK IS DEDICATED
TO

The Adams Family
Three generations—C. F., Weston, Weston, Jr.—who have guided the Bruins on their hockey journeys.

The Bruins Players and Coaches
Who have participated since 1924, some of whom no longer skate on earth.

The Fans
Who have supported the Bruins through the years.

Contents

Opposite: *Weston W. Adams, Frank Weston Adams,
C. F. Adams—first three generations of the Adams family.
C. F. founded the Bruins in 1924 and later turned the
reins over to Weston, who in turn passed the executive
leadership to the fourth generation, his son, Weston, Jr.*

THANK YOU

First, thanks to **Herb Ralby,** who was closely associated with the club from 1933 to 1973. He first covered the Bruins as a reporter with the *Boston Globe,* and later issued reports to the press as the Bruins' public relations man. His memory is vast. His knowledge of the Bruins is even greater.

We would particularly like to thank the people at the Boston Public Library's Print Room and Microtext Department. We are especially grateful for the fine cooperation from **Eugene Zepp.**

We bow our heads with gratitude to **Eddie Lee** and his hidden-away old photos from the dark recesses of the Boston Garden basement.

To **Lefty Reid,** curator of the Hockey Hall of Fame in Toronto, who came through with some needed old photographs.

To **George Collins,** *Boston Globe* librarian, for his assistance in obtaining some *Globe* materials.

To **Chris Maloney,** the right-hand person in Harry's office at the Bruins. She, as usual, was most cordial in making many arrangements.

To **Bob Evans** and **Kevin Connors** of Bobbs-Merrill, who thought the fifty-one years of the Bruins would make a book.

To **Al Ruelle** and all the other well-known photographers. They receive our deepest thanks for permission to reproduce their creative work. Specific acknowledgments are made in each case.

To those of you who might take the time and interest to read this book, we thank you.

Finally, to **Eleanor Grace,** who made countless trips to Boston and spent countless hours researching, note-taking, microfilming, and looking through thousands and thousands of glass negatives, old documents and newspapers. All this good work was almost cancelled out by the parking tickets she managed to pick up!

THANK YOU ALL AGAIN.

C. F. Adams, 1924–1936.

Weston W. Adams, 1936–1969.

Weston W. Adams, Jr., president of the Boston Bruins.

THE ADAMS FAMILY

The Bruins are a three-generations-old tradition in Boston, and the Adams family is an extension of that tradition. We have been inexorably bound to the team, and, for better or for worse, it has been a presence that has totally occupied our lives.

Over the years, I have collected a vault of memories. As the vast array of newspaper clippings, books, magazines and other hockey memorabilia has grown, inevitably my knowledge of hockey has expanded, and my fascination with the sport has tightly held. Rereading the exploits of the early-day Bruins—Eddie Shore, Dit Clapper, Tiny Thompson, Bill Cowley, the Krauts and so many more—always fills me with nostalgia. Statistics tell me that more than five hundred players have worn the Bruins' colors throughout the years.

The Boston teams span over fifty years; they served as the introduction to NHL hockey in the United States.

An integral part of the team's success since 1924 has been somebody we call "a fan"—the pioneer fan who first followed the club when games were skated at the old Boston Arena, and today's Garden fan. He's often loud; he's sometimes overactive; but he's ours and he's loyal! People say Bruin fans are different. They sure are. They've rooted home five Stanley Cup winners and they've supported us throughout the not-so-good years.

The present Bruins are sustaining a hockey tradition in Boston, where tradition and history have been achieved and preserved.

Sport historians thought Eddie Shore so exceptional that he could happen only once in a lifetime. But along came Number 4. Bobby Orr is extraordinary; he can take a commonplace hockey stick and puck and transfer the game of hockey into something artistic. Phil Esposito is another such gifted athlete.

As I have stated, the Bruins have been a major part of my life, and the high moments have to be the 1970 and 1972 teams that produced the Stanley Cup and never-to-be-forgotten memories.

The way I look at it, there are three Bruins teams—those who have played, those playing, and those yet to play.

Some of the Bruins' finest hours have already been clocked in, but I feel many more are yet to come. Memories fade fast, but others are still to be made with Bruins teams of the future.

Weston W. Adams, Jr.

Bobby Orr clutching the 1970 Stanley Cup after his famous goal that gave the St. Louis Blues the real blues in the series final.

INTRODUCTION

Untold words, pictures and stories about the Boston Bruins have been displayed.

The pictures, especially, have been a way of life; things could happen only because they did.

Players spoke. They skated. They acted and reacted.

In this book, people are human. They did good things and sometimes made mistakes.

It has been a long ice skate since 1924.

The Bruins have changed, as we've all changed.

A little bit of time lies buried under the ice of fifty-one Bruins teams.

Hockey has only started. It's only scratched the surface.

Perhaps this book is only a blur on the camera of time, but no history in itself can cover everything. The records of memory flood us with events that happened suddenly and will not be forgotten quickly.

In accepting the years, we are bringing closer a little bit of the past.

Let others make history.

The Boston Bruins already have.

Harry Sinden
Dick Grace

Mr. Hockey, Eddie Shore.

The Beginning

Boston joins big Canadian league

Now has pro team, to be managed by Art Ross. Hub team will play at Arena.

Professional hockey will come to Boston and be played at the Boston Arena this winter. The locals will be called the Boston Professional Hockey Association, Inc., and will be the only American club in the National Hockey League, Canada's foremost group.

The announcement was made last night by President Charles F. Adams of the new pro club and Manager George V. Brown of the Boston Arena.

Brown recently changed his thinking when he tired of the negative interest from the New York hockey backers to promote professional hockey in that big city. This decision gave Boston the opportunity to acquire the players originally headed for New York hockey.

The Seattle team of the Pacific Coast League will be brought here intact by President Adams to represent Boston. Other teams in the National Hockey League are Ottawa, Toronto, Hamilton and two teams in Montreal. One is an English club, playing in a new arena, and the other is the Canadiens, a French team, playing its home games at the Mount St. Royal Rink.

Art Ross, one of the famous figures in Canadian amateur and professional hockey in the last decade, will be manager and vice-president of the team in the Hub.

The league schedule has not yet been drawn up, but President Adams estimates December 1, 1924, as the first game, and the season will run through April.

All teams in the NHL will skate on artificial ice. The local pro team will play about one game a week, although later in the schedule two games a week might be played.

More than likely, Monday nights will be Boston's home nights. To present professional hockey in the right light, extensive improvements will be made at the Boston Arena.

The present rink surface is 220 feet by 90 feet, and Manager Brown intends to condense the area to 190 feet by 80 feet, which is the normal size for a National Hockey League rink.

The costly changes will enable the Arena officials to install 1,000 more seats on the ice level, with a promenade in front.

One of the stipulations in the contract between the Boston Arena and the new professional club is that present amateur players shall not be interfered with in any manner.

Manager Art Ross, former McGill University hockey coach, has assured President Adams that he and his pro players will spend their off hours developing the talent of amateur hockey players in Boston.

The Boston pros informed the press that a schedule committee of the NHL will meet in the near future at Hamilton, Ontario, and a complete game schedule will be released at that time.

Saskatoon claims Boston's Cooper

Western Canada Hockey League's Saskatoon Sheiks made a claim today for Carson Cooper, the Hamilton amateur who is said to be signed by Art Ross and the Boston Professional Hockey Club.

Cooper three years ago accepted a contract with Saskatoon but never reported to the club. He was then placed on a reserve list.

President Frank Calder of the NHL held a meeting in Calgary in 1922 between the Western Canada League and the Pacific Coast League. Results of that meeting pegged Cooper as Saskatoon property.

Mr. Cooper has stated that he wants no parts of Saskatoon and therefore will be placed on waivers by the Sheiks.

Six selected by Boston's pro hockey club

The new players will check in tomorrow at the Arena. The management will start making new ice tonight, and it should be available for practice on Saturday.

Manager Art Ross of the new team is satisfied that his scouting trips through Canada have produced the best possible talent for the Hub team.

Boston pros reported tonight to Manager Ross in Montreal and boarded a train for this city, due here tomorrow morning. President Charles F. Adams of the Boston team announced last night the official list of names on the local squad.

Five crack professionals with established hockey

Art Ross at age eighteen in his younger days in Canada.

reputations will appear on the Boston payroll.

The six amateurs who have turned professional represent some of the cream of the simon-pure players across the border in cold Canada.

Professionals with past experience are Bobbie Rowe, sensational defense player and captain of the Seattle team on the Pacific Coast; Norman Fowler in goal; Bill Harris, a plucky forward; and Skinner, who plays both the forward line and defense. Curley Headley of Saskatoon, a strong defense man, has joined the Hub forces. Manager Ross is trying to obtain Charlie Parkes, another coast veteran with great hockey ways.

Fandom in Canada has been watching with keen interest the efforts of the various professional teams to land Carson Cooper.

Cooper has just given his word to cast his lot with the Boston team. Cooper has been an outstanding scorer in Canadian amateur hockey for the past three years. While with the Hamilton Tigers he led the Ontario Hockey Association in scoring. This big ace should prove to be a real star with Boston.

Other amateurs of great ability from the Hamilton Tigers who will be wearing Boston uniforms are Redding, a good defense man, and Herberts, a Hamilton forward for two years. From Kitchener, Ontario, comes Werner Schnarr. This young man will be remembered by Boston fans as the cog of the Philadelphia team four years ago. He was only seventeen at that time.

Hill and Galbraith are forwards from Eveleth, Minnesota. President Adams stated last night that Manager Ross would look over a half dozen amateurs in next week's workouts. These men come here highly recommended, but since Ross has not seen them he was reluctant to give out any names.

Boston's new pro team will be all set for the opening game with the Saskatoon Sheiks of the Western Division, which is booked in the Arena Thanksgiving night.

November 15, 1924

Boston Bruins in first workout at Arena

The Boston Bruins, new local professional hockey team and a member of the NHL, held their first ice drill of the season this noon at the Boston Arena.

Nothing of a strenuous nature, like a scrimmage, was attempted in the initial meeting. Manager Art Ross, a past master at sizing up the possibilities of a hockey player, worked his men lightly, just enough to get him acquainted with the men and their athletic skills.

Unlike the other professional leaders, Ross was on runners himself. He demonstrated various plays and the correct methods of execution.

Art Ross said, "I appreciate the fact that we don't have too much time to get ready, and I'll really have to work fast with the amateurs."

He noted that there is a vast difference between pro and amateur styles. Professional hockey players skillfully carry through plays with minimum effort; amateur players generally waste lots of energy by useless skating.

Ross's big task for the next two weeks will be to convert the amateurs into big-time professional players.

Two weeks might not be enough, but only time will tell.

Trouble in the hockey world

Schooley claims pros have eyes on his simon-pures.

Once again Pittsburgh is hockey's storm center. This city has two teams in the United States Amateur Hockey Association, the Yellow Jackets, playing in the Western group, and the Pirates, operating in the Eastern wheel.

Manager Roy D. Schooley of the Pittsburgh teams notified the vice-president of the league, George V. Brown, that two professional teams in Montreal, the Canadiens and the Wanderers, have been trying like hell to steal Pittsburgh players.

Schooley is beside himself with anger. One of the important terms in the Boston Arena management contract with the new Boston Professional Team states that all players registered in the United States Amateur Association cannot be touched in any way by the NHL, the professional circuit of which Boston is a member. This signed contract covers all the United States. This is why Schooley's appeal to Vice-President Brown is getting so much notice.

President Charles F. Adams of the Boston Bruins will back Brown to the hilt in the latter's effort to protect amateur hockey in this country.

The Boston professional magnate will be depended upon to use his influence to have the two Montreal pro teams keep their hands off United States amateurs.

An amusing sidelight in connection with Schooley's protest was the fact that the Ontario Hockey Association has made the identical charges for the past three years against the Pittsburgh magnate and his tampering with players from the OHA. Now the skate is on the other foot.

Everyone with hockey knowledge knows that both Pittsburgh teams have players who could make any pro lineup. Schooley has been carefully putting together some strong teams for the past few years. He has won a national title already and has another Pittsburgh club headed that way now.

If he loses his stars he drops out of championship contention, and Mr. Schooley doesn't want that to happen.

Art Ross's Boston Bruins take on Saskatoon Sheiks at Boston Arena tomorrow night

When Bill "Farmer" Cook, professional hockey player, checked in with Art Ross at the Arena yesterday, the Bruins had all their members intact and in shape for the opening professional game with the skating Sheiks from Saskatoon.

Cook's arrival boosted the chances of the Bruins to make an auspicious debut, and, as local Boston papers reported, "Professional hockey could well become higher-class entertainment."

Farmer Cook, from advance notices, was a star in Vancouver, where he played several years as a defense man and was said to be the most accomplished player in pro hockey.

It was reported that he was great on ice and off ice as well. His carefree manner of taking his lumps with a smile made it easy for him to win his way into the hearts of Vancouver hockey buffs.

Working out yesterday at practice with Cook were Hec Fowler, Sailor Herberts, Alf "Dutch" Skinner and Smokey Harris.

It was easy to see that Manager Ross had his men in excellent condition and all set to take the shiny surface against Neway Lalonde's Saskatoon Sheiks.

Bruins management reported, "Although hockey has intruded into the football season, the demand for ticket reservations for the opening game would indicate that the Boston hockey fans are steamed up and will fill the Arena to capacity."

Bruins open career with 2–1 win over Maroons

The new pro team, the Boston Bruins, ventured out into the National Hockey League with an opening victory on Arena ice here in Boston.

It was a pretty good evening's enjoyment for the fans who attended. There were a few empty seats in the place, but it is hoped that they will all be filled, especially when the famous Canadiens come to town.

Some astoundingly harsh checks were delivered to players on both teams. This had an exciting effect on the crowd, who jumped up and yelled for more as the evening swept on.

Punch Broadbent from the Maroons managed to get into a couple of scraps with the Bruins. Referee Mike Rodden had his hands full most of the game trying to keep the teams separated.

Montreal scored first when Charley Dinsmore took a hard shot and picked up his own rebound when the puck dropped off Fowler's pads right in the mouth of the Bruins cage.

Boston made a score when Smokey Harris and Carson Cooper teamed up, with Harris getting the first goal ever scored by a Boston Bruin.

Carson Cooper slid in the second tally unassisted. The Montreal team was a man short at the time, since Mr. Broadbent was serving one of his four penalties of the night.

Lionel Hitchman, Hall of Fame defense man, 1924–25– 1933–34. His number 3 was retired by the Bruins.

◆◆◆◆◆◆

A fan looks back at 1924–25.

Herb Ralby, an early observer of the Boston hockey scene, gives this account of the Bruins' first season:

"Early games at the Boston Arena were especially exciting when the rugged Ottawa Senators came in, with Alex Connell playing goal with his barber-pole-striped jersey and tan linen cap. In those days of the roaring twenties, all the goalies wore caps.

"The Bruins' games were always sold out at the Arena. In fact they had so many sellouts they finally added a balcony. But the viewing wasn't very good, because the old Arena was not designed or built for a balcony.

"Hockey was very popular in the Boston days of the 1920s because of the many amateur teams playing in the area. The non-pros used to pack in good crowds long before the Bruins. They had a shoe-box league. There was quite a scandal when it was discovered that some of the simon-pures were getting paid out of an old cash box or shoe box. Naturally it upset some people because the players were supposed to be strictly amateurs at that time, and money was the root of all evil.

"So many people played for the first Boston team that Art Ross used to tell people he had three teams: one coming, one playing, one going."

◆◆◆◆◆◆

Sprague Cleghorn, in Renfrew uniform before joining the Bruins, 1925–26—1927–28. Member of Hockey Hall of Fame.

The
Roaring Twenties

Bruins scrimmage and fight for team positions

A full squad of Boston Bruins held their first scrimmage of the 1926 season at the Arena today. It proved fierce because the fight for places on the club, which is laden with forwards and defense players, is really tight.

Eddie Shore, the big new defense man from the Western League, was called the best hockey prospect developed in the Patrick circuit last season. He and Lionel Hitchman reported with Sprague Cleghorn yesterday to bring the Bruins to full strength. Shore and Hitchman jumped into practice immediately, but Manager Art Ross sent them to the showers after a brisk half-hour workout.

Duke Keats, Bill Coutu and Dr. Charles Stewart also knocked off after a half-hour.

The new Bruins team is fast and big. No team that played here during the 1925–26 season was as huge as the squad which Ross is directing now.

His defense men are especially large, and there is good solid weight on the forward line. Keats is the heaviest man on the team.

It might be expected that a center ice man weighing 200 pounds was far overweight, but a visit to the dressing room disclosed the fact that Keats's weight is solid, and he will probably go through the year at 195 pounds once he gets into playing shape. Ross has been working out the same combination ideas that made the Bruins such a great passing team a year ago.

Every Bruins forward is a combination man, and the manager stated, "I'll close all practice sessions with forward passing drills. We were good last year with the pass, but this team will be even better."

November 15, 1926

Pro hockey skates off this week

The National Hockey League teams will be divided into groups of five teams. Each club will figure in a week's schedule that calls for twelve games.

The Boston Bruins are in the Western Division, which has as other members the New York Rangers, Pittsburgh, Detroit and Chicago, and will open their season at the Arena tomorrow night with the Montreal Canadiens.

Les Canadiens belong to the Eastern Division, which includes Ottawa, St. Pats, New York Americans and the Montreal Maroons.

The clubs in each section will play each other three times away and three times at home and also meet the other division teams twice away and twice at home.

The league is broken into two groups. Wins and losses will count for and against each team in its own particular section. This schedule was made by the league in order to

give the complete National Hockey League circuit a chance to see all teams in action.

The first three clubs in each division will play off among themselves, the second and third teams meeting first, the winners of this elimination to meet the division leaders later. Then the winners of the two series will clash as divisional champions for the world's professional hockey title.

When the Western League folded, it made it possible for all NHL teams to add experienced players to their rosters.

Every club grabbed as much talent as it could from the defunct circuit.

Professional games at the Boston Arena will be much better than last year, and new faces like Eddie Shore are bound to catch on with the growing hockey public in the Hub.

November 17, 1926

Bruins whack Canadiens 4–1

Boston triumphs in opening ice game. 8,000 fans sit in.

A much better conditioned Boston Bruins team clearly outclassed a slow and sluggish Canadiens club 4–1 last night at the Arena in the opening game of the NHL year.

The Bruins let it be known to the other National League teams that they will have to be reckoned with in the professional ranks this season.

The Bruins team justified all the pre-season reports. They are a fighting, snarling, game team, one that will take nobody's backwash this season.

Last night was not the usual dizzy, dazzling Canadiens of old. The Frenchmen looked as if they were badly in need of vigorous conditioning. The Canadiens were out of shape and failed to show even an occasional flash of their famous passing game.

The Hub club was on top of their opponents from start to finish. Captain Sprague Cleghorn's outfit showed what three weeks of intensive practice can do for a team.

There was just enough rough stuff crowded into the battle to keep the crowd on edge. Penalties were dealt out frequently by referee Jerry LaFlame, and he held a firm upper hand over the entire contest.

The Bruins and Les Canadiens have played better hockey games here, but all things considered, last night's exhibition was surprisingly good under the conditions. The sultry weather of last night took its toll inside the rink. The ice was hard and firm at game time, but it became soft as oatmeal as the battle progressed. A thin fog hung over the surface. Cecil Hart, manager of the Frenchmen, stated after the game, "Conditions here were lousy. I'm going to protest the game to President Calder on account of the bad ice condition."

The protest will not get Hart anywhere, as the league

rules have no clause covering climatic conditions in any specific city on the circuit.

The very mention of a protest is sufficient notice to the sport world that hockey is with us once again. Protests are a way of life for the winter pastime.

The 8,000 fans were satisfied that Archie Briden, Duke Keats, Harry Oliver, Eddie Shore, Billy Coutu and Perk Galbraith are some sweet hockey players. Just the sort of Bruins who will fit into the tough competition that the NHL demands.

Shore made an outstanding impression on all the fans. This big, fine-looking young fellow is fast and tough. He knows hockey and is ever ready to step into the enemy with his 190 pounds. Shore promises to be a star.

Before the contest two live bears were led out on the ice and presented to President Charles F. Adams on behalf of the John T. Connor employees. The bears tugged on their chains and were raring to get started as Bruins official mascots.

"Eagle Eye" Carson Cooper, Bruins right wing, flashier than ever, grabbed all the scoring honors when he caged three goals. Two he scored unassisted, and the other was on a fine pass from Eddie Shore.

Perk Galbraith scored the first goal of the game in the second period when some dumb work by the Canadiens' defense permitted him to shift through and snap a loose puck in for the first counter.

Cooper followed a minute later with his first tally, capturing his own rebound.

Then the dashing Howie Morenz came to life after twelve minutes of play and scored unassisted for the Frenchmen.

Cooper's second goal, scored in the third period, was questionable. Coop took a long shot. The umpire waved his flag indicating a score. The Canadiens protested. This could not be proved by anybody in the press box, situated up near the pigeon's roost. The boys in the press box couldn't peek through the fog on the ice, and besides, they lacked a compass for the proper direction of the rink.

November 23, 1926

Bruins banged in tough battle 2–1
Montreal on top in vicious ice clash. Cleghorn decks Phillips.

In its wildest moments, the Great War was a tea party compared to the mad battle that exploded tonight at Boston Arena, where the world champion Montreal Maroons shot down the Bruins 2–1. The intense war between these teams was re-ignited tonight, and before the game ended, fifteen penalties had been delivered, and referee Bill O'Hara ignored twice that many.

This one lonely referee, however, did a superb job. The trouble lay with the NHL for not assigning two referees to a game between Boston and Montreal, two teams that are on bitter terms.

The game itself was a hell raiser. Sticks were carried high, and there were illegal checks, charging from behind, deliberate socking and countless trips and cross checks that furnished plenty of color and excitement to the evening's outing.

An old battle feud featuring Sprague Cleghorn and Bill Phillips of the Maroons geared up quickly. In passing Phillips at the Bruins net Cleghorn flicked the head of his stick off Phillips's ear. Then Cleghorn immediately took off with a big rush into Montreal territory.

Phillips, standing behind the blue line, hurled his body at the Bruins captain, and the latter was spilled hard. It was the night's severest check. Instantly the play shifted to the Bruins end. Cleghorn once again took the puck from around his net. Phillips poke checked the puck away. As Cleghorn went by Phillips he jabbed the butt end of his stick into the Maroon man and struck him across the face.

Phillips went down and out. Teammates carried the unconscious forward to the Montreal dressing room, where several stitches were required to close his face wounds.

Referee O'Hara assessed Cleghorn with a five-minute penalty. It was only one incident that displayed the game's viciousness. Both sides had many casualties in the hectic battle. Lionel Hitchman was forced out of action with a bruised eye and damaged leg.

Punch Broadbent was carted off, with a bandage on the back of his head where a wild stick had landed with a thump.

At game's end the Montreal and Boston players actually staggered off the ice to the peace and quiet of their dressing rooms.

Out of tonight's carnage emerged one man who has taken Boston fandom by storm. He was the strong Eddie Shore, who normally skates on defense but played right wing during this game.

He later shifted back to defense when Hitch was done in. There may be harder workers, more courageous men, and more tireless skaters in pro hockey than Eddie Shore, but this big youth proved tonight that he is only a few skate strides from stardom with Boston's fandom.

He loves to hit, chase the enemy until they surrender, and then lead the victory parade by his net. Shore is one of those rare irresistible heroes that fans rave about. The flood tide of popularity certainly has covered this Boston Shore.

November 29, 1926

Bruins request two officials for games

Bitterness has developed to a startling degree at this early stage of the season. Major penalties have been dealt to five of the players. The boys are taking the NHL race seriously. That the players who make a livelihood from professional hockey should court banishment, since three of these major fouls may actually result in that, is the wonder and mystery of the sport. Professional baseball and football players cannot understand it.

Hockey is a hard and rugged thing. The NHL rules permit a certain amount of legitimate checking. When a game allows bodily contact with players carrying sticks and wearing keen-edged runners, it requires firm and competent officiating to keep the game within bounds.

The whole trouble lies with the National Hockey League itself. Regardless of conditions in other rinks, two referees are needed to handle NHL games in Boston on the Arena ice.

President C. F. Adams of the Boston Bruins has asked President Frank Calder of the NHL to assign two referees to all future Bruins games here in Boston.

The American Division race finds that the New York Rangers and Pittsburgh are deadlocked on top with the Bruins, an ideal situation with which to steam up the fans.

In the Canadian Division, those hockey masters at Ottawa are out in front.

Aside from Ottawa, it looks as if the class of the NHL will be found in the American Division, where the Bruins have been moving along in the right direction.

November 30, 1926

Ottawa Senators battle Bruins

Professional hockey's masters, the Ottawa Senators, will make their first appearance of the season tonight against the battered and weakened Bruins, who, minus Carson Cooper, will attempt to match their skill against Frank Neighbor's brilliant array of players.

Coop is laid up in bed with a severe attack of the flu. Lionel Hitchman is nursing a bad charleyhorse in his right thigh but expects to dress for the game.

Even if the Bruins were at full strength, they'd have their work cut out for them to stop the flying Senators, who are out front in the Canadian Division. Strange things have happened before, and this might be one of those nights when the Bruins could rise to dizzy heights and knock off Ottawa.

The Senators have gotten the sport of hockey down to a science. They skate with minimum effort. The old football maxim—a good defense is your best offense—fits into Ottawa's thinking. No team has ever skated on NHL ice that can blend defense with attack and get the end results that Ottawa does.

Their starting forward line, with Cy Denneny on left wing, the incomparable Frank Neighbor in center and Hooley Smith on the other wing, represents a trio of pro attackers who are hard to beat. With their attack they also combine defensive qualities that make the going tough for other teams.

Neighbor in center ice is probably the most effective man in forward-line play. His poke check, either a jab or a sweep, has ruined more combination plays than that of any other NHL player. Neighbor rarely goes in close for his shots. He feeds off to his two cracking-good wings, who are both fine shooters.

The Senators also have Jack Adams, Stan Jackson, Hector Kilrea and Frank Gorman for spares.

Opposite:
Eddie Shore's famous
number 2 rests in
permanent retirement.

The great King Clancy, flanked by George Boucher, will be playing on defense.

Alex Connell, the ever-active goalie, will be playing in the nets.

It's a terrific task that faces the Bruins tonight. They realize their weakness without "Hot Shot" Cooper, always a great goal-getter on Boston Arena ice. But you can never tell what's going to happen in pro hockey.

The Bruins management requests that all customers carrying eggs to tonight's contest please park them in the checking room before entering their seats.

December 21, 1926

Fists flare as St. Pats wins

Bruins stung by invaders, who skate over Hub six 5–3.

A straight left to the jaw, which cold-cocked the receiver, and a hailstorm of programs and coins tossed onto the ice were a few of the lively features of the NHL game at Boston Arena tonight when St. Pats from Toronto walloped the Bruins 5–3. Just for the record, it was the first time in the last five games that St. Pats has scored a goal.

A brawl started at center ice when the St. Pats players started misusing referee O'Leary.

Irvin Bailey, St. Pats right wing, standing close to Bruins captain Sprague Cleghorn, was arguing with the latter when the Bruins captain dropped his stick and let go a straight left that landed flush on Bailey's chin. Bailey was flattened, to say the least.

Other players continued to disagree, and the fans joined in by tossing assorted programs and coins onto the ice. Cleghorn went to the penalty box for two minutes, and the ice was scrapped free of debris.

The defeat by St. Pats was the biggest upset of this young season. They came to Boston as a despised tail-ender, with the unenviable record of not having scored a point in the last five games.

However, tonight they were aroused and played all around the Bruins, out-skating, out-yelling, out-everything-ing.

Carson of Toronto made the Boston defense look bad by his well-timed feints and thrusts, which had Boston completely off-balance all night. Carson's three goals in the game sent his total to eight and tied him with Dick Irvin and Babe Dye of Chicago for the league lead.

Eddie Shore contributed some lone dashes and was more spectacular than usual when he landed headfirst in the St. Pats net after scoring Boston's first point.

Back at the bench Shore was asked, "You all right, Eddie?"

Shore grinned. "I'm feeling great. I got a goal."

Percy "Perk" Galbraith, 1926–27—1933–34, another early Bruin Hall of Famer.

December 23, 1926

Bruins take over wild battle 2–1

Players match fists and forget hockey. Stewart gets major for socking.

The Boston Bruins provided an NHL upset here in Montreal tonight when they nosed out the Maroons 2–1 in a wild and weird game by hockey standards.

The Hub club has been handicapped by a long campaign in the past two weeks and looked dull in the early part of the contest. The Christmas season crowd of 7,000 was merry with spirits, and they were all set for an easy Montreal win. But Boston whipped to life and played a fighting game that allowed them to overcome the Maroons' goal by Broadbent. Herberts and Red Stuart got the B's the goals that brought them victory.

Eddie Shore brought the wrath of the fans on his head when he floored the Maroons' center, Nelson Stewart, in a rush on the Boston goal.

It brought a major penalty and a fine to Shore, and a third major of the season to Stewart, which placed him under automatic suspension, subject to the pleasure of the league's president, Frank Calder.

Play swiftly developed into guerrilla warfare in the final minutes, with hardly any good hockey but plenty of tripping, interference, and other illegal procedures.

Sprague Cleghorn took a stick over the eye and later slashed back at Phillips. Cleghorn ended the game with a badly battered eye and bruised feelings. He had plenty to say to Montreal fandom as the Bruins departed from the ice.

April 4, 1927

Yank title for Bruins

Down Rangers 3–1 in New York. Ottawa next for hockey's highest honors.

The Bruins scored three goals in the second period and earned victory with brilliant play by every member of the team. The boys from the Hub will now face the Ottawa Senators in the intergroup series for the Stanley Cup, or what is known as the World Series of Hockey.

Leading by one at the end of the first period, the Rangers allowed themselves to be swept off their steel-shod feet in the second stanza when the two clubs were completely snowed under by an avalanche of penalties. Staggered by this disaster, the New York team was bent, broken and buried by Boston.

The Rangers lost their two defense men, Taffy

Abel and Ching Johnson, when these two beauties claimed the penalty box all for themselves.

The Bruins skated through the remaining on-ice Rangers and wrapped up the contest with three smart goals.

Herberts, Hitchman and Oliver were the Bruins' marksmen. Bill Cook got the one miserable Ranger point.

The game was for a while a free-for-all of tripping, slashing and roughing, and the Rangers can only fault themselves for being led to defeat by a Boston team whose game plan was only too apparent: sucker the New Yorkers into stupid penalties.

However, Eddie Shore spent some time in the delinquent box with two penalties in the first period, four in the second and only one in the third period. Maybe Eddie didn't know the game plan.

Starting Bruins' line-up had Winkler in goal, Shore and Hitchman on defense, Fredrickson at center, Galbraith on left wing and Oliver playing right wing.

Chabot played in the Rangers net, Johnson and Abel played on defense, and Frank Boucher centered for Bun Cook on left wing and his brother Bill on right wing.

April 13, 1927

Ottawa wins title; beats Bruins in deciding game in World Series, 3–1
Sizzling attack sinks B's.

Winter winds are still screaming across the frozen, desolate gray skies of Canada. Out in the boondocks, where villagers wait tensely for news, where loggers huddle around small campfires, word was being carried that old Canada had kept its honor in the first international fight for Stanley Cup prestige.

The Ottawa Senators defeated the Bruins from civilized Boston by the tragic score of 3–1. Now those people in Canada's out-country can sit back, relax, and drink their Canadian whiskey to the likes of Clancy the King, Connell the goalie, Neighbor the Frank, Smith the Hooley, and Denneny, and Kilrea, and Finnigan too. And on and on, drink after drink.

The fourth game of the big series was a harsh windup of a hard, rough series, with stick-belting and fist-swinging. At the closing moments of Game Four even the cops and players had a merry scramble and stumble for five minutes, as the police attempted some order.

Hooley Smith broke Oliver's nose. It was a good thing the game was being held in Ottawa's backyard rink because the Boston fans would never have stood for the Senators' nonsense.

As the game slid into the third period, Shore nailed Kilrea good from the side. Fredrickson started to mess around at the other end of the rink, and Hooley Smith

Aubrey "Dit" Clapper, 1927–28—1946–47. Bruins player, captain and coach. Twenty active years in the NHL and a member of the Hall of Fame. His number 5 has been put aside, never to be worn again by another Boston player.

and Hitchman started swinging sticks. George Boucher rushed to Hooley's aid and mixed with Hitchman as the latter started flinging punches from "down country." Pretty soon the Canadian bobbies bobbled down on the ice and helped restore policeful peace.

The real meanness of the game had not developed as Hooley Smith had yet to do his thing. Now many had considered Hooley a likable guy and one who might even be appreciated in a Boston suit, but as far as popularity goes with Boston fans he is all done—Hooley Smith has had it!

Oliver was riding in to take a pass over the Ottawa line when Smith came from the boards full tilt, hell-bent for no good, and jammed his stick into quiet-loving Harry Oliver's face.

Oliver dropped without a leg or stick under him. Shore rushed up quickly to take over. But poor Eddie was hastened to the cooler before he had a clean chance to belt Smith one and make up for the damage rendered to Oliver.

The injury was later put out as a broken nose, and this nasty piece of work was a cracked climax to a mighty fine hockey season for the 1926–1927 Bruins.

P.S.: Oliver, on an assist from Galbraith, got the only Boston score. It took place in the third period at 17:45, in between scuffles.

November 15, 1927

Babe Ruth watches Bruins-Hawks tie 1–1

Sitting with 9,000 highly enthused hockey fans was baseball's king of swat, Babe Ruth, whose box close by the Blackhawks' bench brought the Babe constant attention from his many admirers. The Babe, as usual, obliged with autographs.

Both teams banged and bumped hard throughout the game. At one point Shore got a nasty toss. He arose like an enraged bull, grabbed the puck and took off with all his speed and might, headed for the Chicago end of the rink, skating over all opposition in his path and sending players sprawling in every direction.

He eventually lost the rubber disc and smashed up against a Blackhawk with the force of a runaway train. Arms, legs, hands and heads were tossed violently into the air, as if from an explosion. The Chicago player shattered against the boards and then fell flat onto the ice. The wonder of it all was that neither was seriously maimed, if not killed.

Hitchman was up to his old puck-stopping tricks. Shore was the same old Eddie, a roaring, dangerous, yet effective player who scared the living hell out of the Chicago boys.

Jim Herberts was the Bruins' hard-luck guy when he had two shots bounce harmlessly off the goal posts.

Sprague Cleghorn was masterful with his checking when the B's were short-handed, which happened on occasion.

Clapper scored the lone Bruins goal unassisted at 12:04 in the second period, after Irvin had knocked one home for the other guys at 12:31 in the first period.

Babe Ruth was seen leaving the game and muttering, "Never saw anything like it. Thank God I'm in baseball, with its peace and quiet."

November 20, 1928

Bruins play first game at new Boston Garden against famous Les Canadiens

The two great teams that wear the colors of the Boston Bruins and Montreal Canadiens will arrive in the Hub this morning, ready for their opening game at the magnificent Boston Garden.

The great Boston Garden, with its arena and amphitheater, will be packed to the high rafters with over 15,000 fans this evening in an ultra setting that only New York with its Madison Square, Detroit with its Olympia and Montreal with its Forum have ever boasted of before to hockey people.

The ostentatious and extremely spacious sporting palace at North Station, a monument to clean sports and clean amusements, was provided with its first ice surface yesterday. A fast sheet of ice will be ready tonight. A busy crew of hard workers has installed side boards, painted them white, and marked out the well-known "blue lines."

The nets, designed by Art Ross, were new and untested and leaned lazily against the boards.

The Garden playing surface is bigger than the Boston Arena by some five or ten feet. This might be a thing to consider when the Canadiens' Frenchmen, Howie Morenz, Joliat and Gagnon, start flying down the ice with their speed and clever stick-handling.

C. F. Adams of the Bruins has requested that the NHL send Montreal to Boston for the grand opening of the Garden. Montreal can always draw a crowd, which will help in dedicating the Bruins' new rink.

Herb Gardiner is gone from the Canadiens and has been replaced by Marty Burke, the fiery lad brought up from Pittsburgh. "Big Boy" Mantha, a real Bruins pest, will be at his old defense post for the flying Frenchmen.

The Bruins are expecting big things from Cooney Weiland, obtained from Minneapolis just a year ago. Young Weiland is said to be one-hundred-percent ready for the pros, a superstar, so to speak, and could become a big Boston favorite before long.

Two new Bruins numbers had to be created for "Baby" Klein and Cy Denneny. The Klein kid is only eighteen, with 185 pounds of bone and muscle. He's bound to be another Eddie Shore. "Baby" doesn't know his own strength and in recent practice had the other Bruins "laying off" him, which is a real compliment. Like Weiland, he's another discovery of the new year. The Boston fans certainly remember Ottawa's Cy Denneny. He now skates with Bruins number 16 on his back and has been appointed Art Ross's assistant on the bench. Cy will still take his regular turn on the ice. Denneny's a real pro and can handle himself on and off the ice.

Dutch Gainor will more than likely be sidelined for the gala opener. After last season, Dutch ducked into the hospital for a couple of quick operations on his legs and face.

All the old favorites will be back for the 1928–1929 campaign. Eddie Shore and Lionel "Big Three" Hitchman will be stationed on defense. Shore has always been the rip-roaring type, while Hitch plays it a little cooler but knows all there is to know about defense.

Harry Oliver and Perk Galbraith, the wings, are in better form than last year and are anxious for the first faceoff. Fredrickson at center has promised to go all out with no stops.

The old reliable Hal Winkler or the new rookie "Tiny" Thompson will be starting in the strings tonight.

From all indications, tonight's first tilt will be a sellout. The Garden doors will open at seven o'clock, an hour and a half before game time, to give the fans a chance to wander through the new sports palace and find their seats.

Fifteen hundred seats will go on sale for fifty cents to bring big league hockey into the range of everyone's purse. When all seats are sold, 5,000 extra admissions will be available at a buck a throw. Boston's new Garden establishes the Hub as the NHL's hottest location.

There will be practically no formal opening, as President C. F. Adams of the Bruins does not like fancy affairs such as they have had in other NHL cities. He feels that the Boston fans are too intelligent for such ballyhoo stunts and that they want their hockey straight and hard, as only the Bruins can play.

Harry Oliver, 1926–27—1933–34, Hall of Fame member.

November 21, 1928

Les Canadiens cop opening Garden fray with Mantha's goal 1–0
17,000-plus jam big new Garden.

Thousands of fans, coming even from Cape Cod, expected to be accommodated with Bruins tickets at the last minute.

They crowded the Garden entrances, ran against the gates, and smashed windows and doors in the craziest scene ever witnessed at any Hub event.

Security guards, caught unaware, were trampled as the giant waves of humanity kicked and fought their way to the Garden. Women were overcome and fainted, and it was not until an emergency call was made for extra Boston police that the frenzied mobs dispersed. Paid ticket holders got caught in the rush and were tossed aside in the mad scramble for admission to the game.

President C. F. Adams arrived on the scene and ordered all doors to be opened to prevent a disaster.

Inside, the famous American Legion Band from Weymouth was knocking out lively tunes to calm the ruffled situation.

It was a night to remember when the 17,000-plus rose in a body and sang the American and Canadian national anthems.

Some of the younger element climbed high up on the rafters to gain perches so they could look directly down on the ice.

When the opening faceoff took place, a roar went up that lasted for a full five minutes.

Outside, the demand for admittance continued, and the impatient lines of pushing, fighting people extended around the new North Station office building and down to the Warren Avenue Bridge.

President Fuchs of the Boston Braves baseball team sent a huge floral piece with best wishes to the Bruins. This was carefully placed in the Bruins' shower to keep it cool and fresh.

Prominent people in the boxes and front seats were dressed in evening clothes and dress wraps. They had partied all over Boston before the game and had come to witness the great sports spectacle.

The game itself was a good one, with lots of scrapping and tremendous skating as these opponents of the last two years swapped strategy and carried the puck up and down the ice.

Mantha lugged the disc from his own defense, stood Lepine as a decoy on the right wing, split the B's defense and whacked a terrible shot home just above the knees. The lightning blast hit Tiny Thompson on the right leg as he threw it out to defend, but the puck bounced off his leg into the corner of the net.

Next time you're asked, "Who scored the first goal at Boston Garden?" be sure to answer, "Mantha of Montreal." The prestige remains with his name.

17

December 4, 1928

Myles Lane from Melrose replaces Ching Johnson as World Champion Rangers battle Bruins

Melrose's Myles Lane's big night will come when he steps on the new Garden ice as a New York Ranger. Lane is no stranger to Boston fans; in the past, they have turned out in tremendous numbers to witness encounters between his Dartmouth College Indians and John Harvard at the Arena. Melrose's super athlete was also well known on the football field as an all-American back.

Lane will replace Ching Johnson, who was bunged up last Sunday with a possible cracked bone in his ankle.

Taffy Abel, the other veteran Ranger defense man, is laid up with a bum shoulder, so Lane in his Garden debut will be called upon for lots of extra ice time.

Lane isn't yet another King Clancy but he is heading in the right direction. Lane has had plenty of football experience and relishes physical contact. He is one guy who knows how to take the heaviest kind of punishment.

The New York club features the high-powered, smooth-working line of Bad Bill Cook at right wing, brother Bunny on left, and Frank Boucher at center.

Manager Art Ross broke his long-standing rule when he ordered the B's out for a full hour's workout on the day of a game. Usually the players rest

to conserve their energy for the evening's main event.

Advance ticket sales for this game have been extraordinary, and a huge crowd is expected to beat down the Garden's doors. Bruins ticket windows opened at 9 A.M., and the usual 1,500 tickets at fifty cents went on sale on a first come, first served basis. When all reserved seats were sold, a limited number of standing rooms were placed on sale.

The Rangers will arrive by train this afternoon, and Garden doors will open at 7 P.M.

The Boston and Maine Railroad will run three special trains carrying hundreds of out-of-town fans to the big game. The Gloucester special will leave at 6:57 P.M., the Haverhill special goes at 7:15, and Manchester will chug along at 6:30, all due to arrive at North Station around 8:00.

December 5, 1928

Myles Lane visits Hub, but Bruins topple New York 2–0
Melrose lad shows great poise.

The Bruins came into their own in their new Garden when they whipped the fearless Rangers 2–0 before a sellout crowd estimated at better than 17,000, not including all the sneak-ins.

Myles Lane from Melrose, the Dartmouth star, showed for the first time and drew his share of cheers from the heavy Melrose-Dartmouth tinge of Greater Boston fans.

Lane has learned his trade fairly well, as he was chased to the penalty box three times during the evening's outing.

Ching Johnson was out with a broken leg, and Taffy Abel, the other Ranger defense man, was on the disabled list.

Melrose Myles was quite sharp on defense and did his damnedest to be a Ching Johnson on attack as he lugged the rubber down the ice on several New York rushes. Each time he took off, the crowd stood and applauded.

However, the Rossmen scored in the second and third periods. Cy Denneny, the cagey old master, knew just where to be when Eddie Shore made one of his locomotive dashes that had the Garden spectators beside themselves. Shore cracked a hard one off the back dasher that flipped in front of the net, where Denneny was waiting to click it home over goal tender Roach's shoulder.

Harry Oliver was outstanding and earned the featured-player selection of the night. He is now being compared favorably with the Cook brothers of New York and Joliat from Montreal.

With this kind of recognition, it was no surprise when Oliver got the second Boston goal.

The customers got their usual treat from Eddie Shore, who seemed to be feeling well enough to take an extra turn or so down the ice. Every time Shore wound up, the crowd would jump up.

Young Cooney Weiland looked good. He skated all over the place, never stopped, and used expert judgment.

Hitchman, with his long poke check, and some of the other Bruins appeared anxious to test Myles Lane and see how much the big football star could stand.

He stood up quite well but was seen after the game quietly packing his bumps and bruises into a new traveling bag given to him by his Melrose fans.

Myles Lane from Melrose, Massachusetts, and Dartmouth College. Member of Bruins, 1933–34.

◆◆◆◆◆◆◆

December 1928 . . . . . Bruins picked up ace in Weiland. Cooney's hockey sense makes a big hit in Boston.

Weiland spoke, "If you think I deserve a story, you might say that I'm the only one from my hometown playing pro hockey."

Cooney hails from Edmondville, near Seaforth, Ontario, a rural one-blacksmith, one-post-office hamlet of 2,000.

The young Bruin was twenty-four when he joined the team. He weighed 150 pounds and stood 5 feet, 7 inches.

Weiland says he got his nickname "Cooney" when he was seven or eight, riding in a buggy with an older man. The buggy driver was chewing something, so Weiland asked him for some. The man bit off a chew and handed it to Weiland, who plunged it into his mouth and immediately got black in the face and green in the stomach. The older man had a great laugh at Weiland's plight and spread the story all over Edmondville, calling Weiland "Cooney."

But the name "Cooney" became famous not from eating but from hockey.

The young Bruin's powerful build was developed from pole-vaulting and high-jumping in his high school days, when he won several first prizes. He also had his early athletic hand in baseball and lacrosse.

Bruins fans especially appreciated Weiland's effectiveness in attacking and back checking. He had an uncanny way of swinging his stick to break up a play with complete accuracy and control, to the great dismay of all Bruins opponents.

Art Ross pulled a real ace when he yanked Weiland from the American Association to the Bruins.

◆◆◆◆◆◆◆

December 11, 1928 . . . . . C. F. Adams's telegram.

Colonel John Hammond, New York Rangers president, sent a wire to Mr. Adams: "Myles Lane has given us all the publicity we had hoped for. His heart and public are in Boston. Would you consider his trade for Shore?"

Immediately Bruins President C. F. Adams wired back: **"You are so far from Shore you need a life preserver."**

◆◆◆◆◆◆◆

December 26, 1928 . . . . . Fredrickson thanks Boston fans in letter to newspapers.

To the Hockey Fans of Boston:

Leaving the ranks of the Boston Bruins is to me a keen disappointment, but "every cloud has a silver lining," and the silver lining of my dark cloud was revealed in the many kind words and solicitations received from many hockey fans and followers with whom I have come in contact since the news of my transfer to the Pittsburgh Pirates.

I will always cherish in my memory the privilege of having had the opportunity of knowing something about Boston and Bostonians.

◆◆◆◆◆◆◆

January 3, 1929

Shore Beats Maroons 1–0

Eddie Shore scored the game's only goal in the second period.

Montreal was caught short, with Stewart and Hicks cooling their heels in the penalty box. Stewart was in for a major after striking Dutch Gainor over the head with his stick.

After the game the same Mr. Stewart was fined fifty dollars for having passed several uncomplimentary remarks to referee O'Leary as the latter skated off the ice.

One Stewart booster, after hearing about the fine, yelled after O'Leary, "Boy, have you got sensitive ears."

It still cost Nels Stewart the fifty bucks.

◆◆◆◆◆◆◆

January 3, 1929 . . . . . Eddie Shore's motor trip to Montreal.

The Bruins' train for the Montreal game of January 3 left North Station at 8:45 P.M. on January 2. The Bruins' private car, a sleeper, was usually the last car on the train.

This particular night, Eddie Shore was having dinner with friends in Brookline before heading for North Station to catch the train.

A monstrous traffic jam on the way to the station caused Shore to arrive late, just as the Bruins' train was pulling out. Shore gave chase down the tracks, but sometimes even trains are faster than Eddie.

How to get to Montreal? Shore's well-heeled Brookline pal offered him his car and chauffeur.

Outside of Boston they ran into a blizzard and ice-covered roads.

The chauffeur had trouble keeping the car on the slippery roads, and Shore asked him, "Have you had any experience driving on snow and ice?" The man shook

his head. Shore, who was from the snow country of Western Canada, said, "Well, I have. Let me take the wheel." He drove the rest of the night.

The next morning, deep in Vermont and nearing the Canadian border, the exhausted Shore handed back the driving to the chauffeur with the admonition, "Drive slowly," and he quickly curled up in the back seat. A few minutes later Shore felt the car sliding all over the road, and he climbed back into the front seat to make sure the driver kept the speed down to about twenty miles per hour. The car still slid and finally ended up off the road in a ditch.

Shore hurried to the nearest building, looking for help. Finally he located a garage. There was no tow truck available, only an old hearse. Eddie took it, hitched it to the car and yanked the vehicle from the ditch.

Once again Shore and his driving pal were off and running. They arrived in Montreal around 5 P.M. of the afternoon of January 3. He spotted Dit Clapper and Cooney Weiland in the hotel lobby, coming back from their pre-game meal and going up for a nap.

"I know you guys will be getting up at six," Shore told them after recounting his all-night drive. "I'm going to hit the sack for an hour; wake me when you get up."

Clapper and Weiland called Shore at six, but Eddie continued to sleep on from complete exhaustion. The Bruins' players doused Eddie with cold water, which got a quick rise out of him, and off they went to the Montreal Forum.

That night, with his eyes looking like pinholes in the snow after the long drive and sleepless night, Shore scored the only goal in the game for the Bruins' 1–0 victory.

Art Ross rewarded Eddie with a five-hundred-dollar fine for missing the train.

◆◆◆◆◆◆◆

Frank Fredrickson, 1926–27—1928–29. Elected to Hall of Fame.

pened to play. I must have played a hundred games while trying to fall asleep. Plays were going this way and that, and I tried to figure them all out. I got up in the morning exhausted and I hoped that I could eat properly during the day and help set myself for the game. But everything I ate jumped up and down, and the excitement of it all had me on edge until I heard the whistle blow, and then I calmed down."

The new Bruins player continued, "Playing pro hockey with the Bruins is something. You don't have much time to think. The pros are in and away and back again, and how they can skate, pass and stick-handle."

Eddie Shore was over in the corner getting dressed when he was asked, "What do you think of George?"

"Think of him?" came Shore's reply. "Holy smoke, he's a pip. Just as soon as he caught on out there, and it happened all like that, I didn't have a thing to worry about. Did you see him . . . ?" And Shore went on with a whole list of great things that George Owen had done in the game.

Art Ross, Bruins manager, was asked his opinion of Owen. "What are you asking me, riddles?" said Ross. "You don't think that I've been breaking my neck for four years trying to land this bird for the Bruins and then have him figured out all wrong, do you? I'm tickled to death at his showing, and I don't mean maybe."

Evidently George Owen had really arrived in his very first game as a Bruin.

Opposite: *Harvard's George Owen graduated to the Bruins as a player, 1928–29—1932–33.*

January 9, 1929

George Owen plays in first Bruins pro game

Owen admits he was nervous.

"Like it?" said Owen in answer to a fan's question. "Why, I love it. Tonight's game, that's what I call real hockey. I'm glad you think I did okay, but who couldn't do a good job with such forwards as I had to work with? Those guys took all the burden off me."

That was George Owen and his modesty. Owen played a fine defensive game his first time out as a Bruin.

In answer to another question about his big pro game against Toronto, Owen said, "I felt just like I did in my sophomore year going against Yale. That was my first big shot in sports, and I was some worried." He went on, "All last night I had it on my mind what I would do if I hap-

Marty Barry, Bruins member who skated with the team from 1929–30 to 1934–35. Hall of Fame member.

22

To Fred
Georges Owen

March 16, 1929

Bruins end season beating Pirates 3–1
Players presented watches by fans.

The Bruins set an NHL record by winning the game against Pittsburgh. They annexed their twenty-sixth victory, beating an old Ranger mark by one game.

Tiny Thompson, in front of the Boston twine, played a very nonchalant game. His style was free and easy. That gave the fans several laughs all night long. Tiny said after the game, "I used to have that same relaxed feeling before I joined the pro ranks. The strain of other hard games this year has been making me fight the puck, so to speak, just like a baseball infielder does under pressure."

A home-bred Bostonian, Bill Stewart, got a big hand when his name was called as referee. This was his first shot at big-time hockey in Boston, although he has worked other NHL cities.

Weiland had a great night with his expert sweep checking, and Owen, as usual, was giving no end of bother to the other team.

Myles Lane also saw Bruins action, which gave the local fans something to yell about.

Once again it was the stunning work of Eddie Shore that accounted for the Bruins' record win. Shore rapped home the third goal when he stopped Drury flat in his tracks with a poke check, wound up, decked two rival forwards in the center zone, cracked a path between the points, recovered on the inside and pasted a screamer by Miller, the Pirates' goal tender.

Ralph "Cooney" Weiland, Boston player, 1928–29—1931–32; 1935–36—1938–39. He also served the Bruins as a coach.

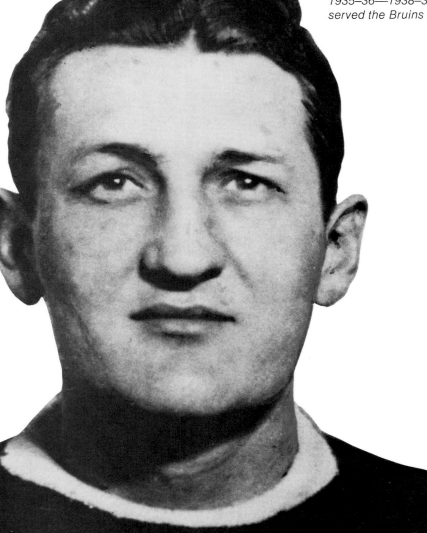

March 22, 1929

Bruins, aroused to frenzy by Canadiens' two-goal lead, play inspired hockey to win

Hitchman blooded. Shore wild. Ross emotional. Players ride party train to Hub.

Les Canadiens were knocked off in such a slick manner by the Bruins that the Stanley Cup seems only down the bend in the road, waiting and ready to find a home in old Bean Town, which has been waiting three years to qualify. The Flying Frenchmen, real terrors when hockey is the word, were completely surprised when the desperate Rossmen, who never quit for a second, reached out and knocked the Canadiens cold.

As far as can be remembered, at least since the Bruins have mingled in NHL hockey, no other team has ever barged through playoff opponents in three straight games.

The Bruins were led by their courageous captain Hitchman, who feared nothing, and whose spirit infuriated the hot-tempered Frenchmen. Blood streamed all over Hitchman's face from a tremendous gash on his head. Later in the game, the same wound was opened up again by another high stick, and he constantly wiped blood from his eyes and mouth. He obeyed Ross's shouts of "Stay on the ice! Don't get any penalties!" Finally Hitch swung over to the Bruins' bench and asked, "Art, how much longer have I got to put up with this stuff?"

The cool Ross, who never batted an eyelash, was sitting quietly, studying the play. Slowly his anger was building as he watched the condition of his men and their wounds. The first goal brought a slight lift to Ross's brow, the second a smile, and the third by Eddie Shore had Ross up out of his seat like a firecracker, throwing his fist through the air.

An ambition in Art Ross's long career had finally been realized. He had beaten a great team in his own hometown—Montreal.

Howie Morenz was the first Canadien over to congratulate the Bruins after the final bell. Ross showed his true emotion by leaning over the fence and wrapping Morenz's shoulder with his arms. "You are a great hockey team, Howie," the excited Ross exclaimed.

It was like a bunch of kids on Christmas morning in the Bruins' dressing room, and the league of mutual admiration was going from player to player.

Cecil Hart, Les Canadiens' manager, and Leo Dandurand, the managing director, along with Herb Gardiner and other Canadien players, crowded into the Bruins' quarters with

Cecil "Tiny" Thompson, Bruins goal tender, 1928–29— 1938–39. Four-time winner of the Vezina Trophy for goal tender with best goals-against average. Hockey Hall of Fame.

their best wishes. English and French flowed with the bubbly.

All the way to Boston from Montreal, people gathered at little stations to wave and shout to the passing train carrying the Bruins back to the Hub. It was like the American army returning from overseas after the Great War.

March 24, 1929

Bruins ovation is mighty; North Station welcome is wild

Players cheered, mobbed, hugged after victory over Montreal.

The greatest reception ever recorded for a Boston team found a lively and enthusiastic crowd of hockey followers swarming around the Boston Bruins last night at North Station.

The Bruins were battle-weary from the Montreal games. They were tossed around by a crowd of fans who pushed their way through a large detail of Boston police.

A half-hour before the Bruins' train arrived from Montreal, the crowd began to overflow the vast new train depot. The Boston papers had covered the Montreal game in full detail, and people were still talking about the Bruins

goals that were jammed through within six minutes of each other to bring the big Bruins victory.

The players had no idea about the reception awaiting them. But when the train pulled in and the Bruins slid open the doors, they saw the huge throng. Captain Hitchman was the first off the train and led the team down the platform through the gates to a scene that the players will never forget.

Hitch had most of his face covered with bandages to hide his Montreal hockey wounds.

The great crowd started to yell, "We want Hitchman! We want Eddie! Hey, hey, where's Cooney Weiland?" And again came the cry, "C'mon, Tiny! Step up there, Thompson!"

Something gave way. The ropes bulged, the crowd packed in and the police were shoved good-naturedly out of the way.

Bruins' backs were slapped, hands shaken. The fans were getting a first-hand look at their heroes.

Frank Ryan, the hockey voice of the Bruins on radio, took a hand, piled up some luggage, and yelled to the mass of humanity. The fans needed direction, and he was the guy to be their leader. Ryan called for cheers for all the players and finally for Manager Art Ross.

The organized rooting gave the police time to adjust their thoughts and plans, and with pleadings to the public, they opened a pathway for the Bruins, who ran to waiting cabs.

The players knew that their beating powerful Montreal three straight games had really made a big hit with their fans.

"I bet there are a lot of good defense men in this crowd," said Hitchman as his path was blocked time and again.

"Yes," said Tiny Thompson, "and I can stop those French Canadiens, but I'll be damned if I can keep this gang off my back."

"I don't know if this is rougher than hockey," yelled Eddie Shore, pushing his way into a taxi. "I expect to get the makings of another cocoon on my eye to match the one I have."

The people stayed on after the Bruins left North Station, discussing the big night's homecoming for the Stanley Cup Bruins.

Unfortunately, Art Ross missed the whole thing, as he remained behind in Montreal with his family and wasn't present at the great demonstration of hockey fandom in Boston.

One of the last Bruins to jump into a cab was the center of all eyes, little Ralph "Cooney" Weiland. Someone who knew something yelled from the crowd, "Hi, Cooney, where's the wife?"

"We've kept it a secret pretty long," Weiland finally mentioned. "None of the guys on the team had the slightest idea we were married until they read it in Sunday's paper. Art Ross knew about it, but Gertrude and I made Art promise to keep it a secret."

Weiland's bride is the former Miss Gertrude E. Hussey of Minneapolis. They were married in Boston on March 6, 1929. Pretty soon they may be able to get away on a honeymoon, but, as Cooney related, "First things first, and that's the Rangers. We've got to take care of them."

March 29, 1929

Bruins win. Beat Rangers 2–1 in final clash for Stanley Cup
B's goals by Oliver and Carson.

A five-year quest for Lord Stanley's big cup ended here tonight at Madison Square Garden, where the Bruins captured the prize they have sought so long by beating the Rangers 2–1. This was the second and last game of the finals.

Along with the hard-earned victory went the record for the shortest Stanley Cup series since the method of elimination games was devised by the NHL.

The final game was bitterly fought for a full sixty minutes without a moment's letup. The Rossmen gave their utmost to outplay the desperate Rangers club.

It was a game of thrills, sustained action, speed and checking which few games in the 1928–1929 season could equal. The paid admissions got their money's worth in this one.

Oliver was a flash all night, and Dr. Bill Carson was the man of the hour, knocking home the winning puck. When it appeared that the game might go into overtime, Oliver whistled down the right lane, with Carson following in the center. At the points, Carson caught a pass, whizzed around Johnson as Ching dived at him, and flung home a beauty that hung the strings in back of Roach, the Rangers' goal tender, for the goal that gave the Bruins the Stanley Cup.

Carson's tally came at 18:02 of the third period, and for the rest of the contest the Rangers swarmed in front of the Bruins' net, trying to get back into the game. However, super defensive work by the Rossmen kept the Rangers off the scoreboard until the Boston rooters were able to send up a lusty and mighty cheer as the old bell clanged, ending the series.

Bruins hold annual "bust"

Showered with gold after Stanley Cup season. Start vacation vocations.

What do the Bruins do off season? Well, Tiny Thompson will be playing baseball. Eddie Shore will resume farming, and George Owen goes back to banking.

Last night the Bruins held a gala affair at the Copley Plaza Swiss Room, where a miniature hockey rink, complete with goals, blue lines and all, was built for the festive occasion.

President C. F. Adams acted as toastmaster and Santa Claus as he divided up $35,000 in player bonuses.

Each Bruin received $500 in gold for winning the Stanley Cup, which was prominently displayed with the Prince of Wales Trophy.

Players, club management and hockey writers were all invited to hear the Honorable James M. Curley as the featured speaker. A handsome silver chest was given to the new bridegroom Cooney Weiland and his wife.

The players presented owner Adams with a two-foot bronze bear imported from Russia.

Captain Lionel Hitchman had the puck that scored the final goal against the Rangers mounted on a silver plaque and inscribed with all the Bruins' names.

Manager Art Ross was presented with a registered set of golf clubs and a golf bag.

Mr. William Cole, a prominent confectioner, gave all present a box of candy, so the affair did end on a sweet note, despite Art Ross's diet.

The 1928–1929 season of forty-four games and five play-offs were already in the record books, and the players arrived at the party in wonderful condition. It is said that they departed the party in even better condition—so to speak.

Before the party broke up, it was learned that Thompson was going back to playing ball with the Claresholm club in Alberta. Naturally, he plays first base to keep his catching hand in shape. After the baseball season ends, he will spend a couple of weeks on a Canadian wheat farm before reporting to training camp.

Dutch Gainor, the famous zig-zag man, will again be a shortstop on the same team with Tiny.

Eddie Shore is a big wheat and real estate man up Edmonton way, and Number 2 is headed back on that route again. In 1928 Eddie purchased a farm, complete with thrashing machines, and he plans to keep busy down on the farm until the autumn leaves start to fall. Shore had a great year in 1928–29 and said at the party, "I'm in much better shape than a year ago, but that's not counting tonight."

James Lloyd Klein, the Bruins' kid and a semi-pro

The great offensive defense man, Eddie Shore.

pitcher for Saskatoon, will have Myles Lane running around in the outfield in the same old Eastern League. Lane said, "I hope to sign on as a backfield coach in the fall, before hockey starts again."

Dit Clapper reported he was going to spend his time selling cars to people with raccoon coats and hip flasks.

Cooney Weiland, who has been a druggist other summers, will spend the summer with his wife, traveling throughout Minnesota.

The clever right winger Harry Oliver will work as an electrical engineer in Winnipeg.

Perk Galbraith is a lumber man in Oliver's hometown.

Bill Carson will continue as a dentist, yanking teeth in Toronto.

Cy Denneny worked for the Canadian government in the Geodetic Survey from Ottawa and will continue those duties.

The Bruins' cattleman, Mickey Mackay, will be on a ranch in British Columbia.

Lionel Hitchman dabbles in insurance but said, "I will have a good long rest and just vacation in the wild bush country, slapping mosquitoes most of the summer."

George Owen, a rapid sensation who made his first appearance in pro hockey in 1929, will work as a banker here in Boston this summer.

Manager Art Ross plans to keep active playing golf around Montreal, shooting in the low seventies. The year before, Ross worked for the Boston Braves as traveling secretary. However, since January 1928 he has been on a strict diet and clearly stated he is going to watch his weight.

Thus the "bust" ended a season that certainly was not a bust, because the Bruins carried home the bacon with the Stanley Cup.

November 23, 1929

Bruins win see-saw game with Maroons

Montreal ties Bruins twice but loses 4–3. Eddie Shore knocked down and out.

Dave Trottier, Maroon left winger, scored in the first period, and a goal by Weiland, assisted by Shore, tied the score. Hooley Smith put Montreal on the scoreboard again in the second period.

Boston, with a great display of the newly permitted forward pass, snapped three quickies past Benedict, the tallies coming from Carson's, Weiland's and Clapper's sticks. Stewart of Montreal put one away in the final period, but it was still one shy of a tie.

Eddie Shore, who played a dynamic game, was knocked heavily to the ice near the end of the game and had to be assisted off the ice, leaving the surface stained with his blood. Babe Siebert, who made the check, was not penalized, the referee ruling it a legal bump.

In this contest Shore suffered a broken nose, three bashed teeth, two black eyes and thirteen facial stitches.

Preceding page:
Boston Bruins, 1928–29 Stanley Cup champions.
Front row: Harry Oliver, Mickey Mackay, Bill Carson,
Cooney Weiland, Perk Galbraith, Dutch Gainor
Back row: Tiny Thompson, Eddie Shore, George Owen,
Harry Connor, Marty Barry, Dit Clapper, Lionel Hitchman,
Art Ross (Manager)

Opposite:
Early photograph of a Bruins game in the 1930s, with
unusual Garden lighting.

The
Depression Thirties

January 12, 1930

Bruins' winning streak broken

Americans launch attack, tally three goals. Cop game 3–2.

The wild New York Americans played a well-disciplined defensive game and broke the fourteen-game winning streak of the Boston Bruins, champions and leaders of the NHL, with a hard-earned 3–2 victory.

The unexpected triumph was all the more remarkable because it was the second in two nights for the Amerks, tailenders of the International group.

Now the B's have to start winning all over again.

January 1930

Headguards for Bruins

Ross concerned about players' safety after Montreal Maroons' dirty work.

Usually, after a hockey game is played it is quickly forgotten. But last night's game in Montreal was different.

During the train ride back to Boston, the Bruins chewed over the Maroons and their intentionally treacherous habits. Some of the Bruins called the game the meanest since 1924.

Mentioned as chief villains were Hooley Smith and Dave Trottier.

Not once did the B's brag about, "We'll get them good at the Garden."

Eddie Shore said, "I've only been in a couple of real donnybrooks that were nearly as bad."

One of the Bruins recalled when Irving Small of the B.A.A. amateur days was assaulted with a stick by a Berlin, Germany, player. The Bruins went on to say, "Last night was a helluva lot worse."

The reporters covering the game and riding on the Bruins' train couldn't get over the deliberately dirty playing by Montreal.

Art Ross issued a statement: "You can bet that my defense men will all wear helmets on the next game here in Boston."

In the Maroon game, Hooley Smith whaled Hitchman over the head. It was a good thing Hitch was wearing a helmet because it could have been serious. Since Hitchman broke his jaw he has been using a headpiece as part of his regular equipment.

Mr. Smith received only a two-minute minor for the infraction.

This was also the same Mr. Smith who broke Harry Oliver's nose in another Ottawa game. On that same night, after the game, Hitchman chased Hooley Smith out of an after-hours eatery down the early-morning streets of darkened Ottawa.

Evidently Smith hadn't forgotten that running engagement when he went after Hitchman with his stick in hand.

Trottier also had bad intentions for Hitchman, as he attempted to mash Lionel's face with his stick. Hitchman turned in time to take the swung stick on the arm but had to leave the game for repairs.

The Bruins reported that not too much could be expected from the officials on hostile Montreal ice, where the French fans whip themselves into a bitter frenzy that stirs the Maroons' blood. They screamed during the whole game and shouted constant threats to the officials. It was mob rule in the Montreal game.

Stewart and Trottier spent the entire evening trying to give Shore the business every chance they got.

One time, Stewart gave Shore the elbow, then the stick, skating innocently off while Trottier gave Eddie the high stick too. When Shore ducked, Trottier took the opportunity to drag his stick over Shore's skull. Shore played it cool and didn't lose his temper, but opened his arms like a boxer and "broke clean."

The Bruins were rugged. When they hit, they hit hard, but there was no deliberate meanness about them. They tripped and held and did other interesting things, but yet they were not vicious. When they adopt such measures they will be certain to lose face with the Boston fans, who want fair play from their team.

Eddie Shore.

March 28, 1930

Dutch Gainor lost to Bruins—goes to hospital

Dutch Gainor, popular left winger of the Boston Bruins, was shipped to the hospital yesterday afternoon for an operation at 5 P.M. He couldn't make it to the Garden for last night's game.

EDITOR'S NOTE: I wonder why he didn't show up?

December 25, 1930

Free-for-all at Garden; Bruins win 8–0
Players riot. Police called.

The mammoth brawl was started by Hib Milks after he was legally checked by George Owen of the Bruins. The only player on the ice not to take part was Petch Cude, the Philadelphia goal tender, who evidently was having enough excitement just playing in the nets and trying to keep out of the way of the Bruins' eight goals.

It was Christmas, but there was no peace on ice and good will toward hockey players last night at Boston Garden.

This was the largest fight on Boston ice since the infamous egg-tossing game back at the Arena in 1925. This was a real old-style knock 'em down, pick 'em up, knock 'em down again, with everyone taking a swipe at the man nearest to him, teammate or not . . . as long as someone got conked.

Even the referee, Mickey Ion, and the linesman, Bill Shaver, took a couple of solid whacks on the chin before peace was finally restored by the gallant Boston police, under the stern supervision of Superintendent Michael Crowley.

It was so wild that the police suggested calling the marines from the nearby Charlestown Naval Base, but nobody took that suggestion seriously.

Funny thing—the Philadelphia team operates under the peaceful name of the Quakers.

Back to the fight. Milks was hurrying down the ice with every good intention of shooting at the Boston net when handsome George Owen stepped into his path. Milks was naturally quite disturbed by the imposition and swung his stick in the direction of Mr. Owen, who then proceeded to flatten Milks with a Harvard football tackle.

Eddie Shore came to Owen's rescue, and Wally Kilrea joined forces with Milks.

Christmas was the order of the day, but nevertheless, all good friendship disappeared as sticks and gloves were discarded. Dit Clapper, with three goals for the night, not only was the leading scorer but did quite well in taking

out Wally Kilrea too—one left jab and one right cross put Kilrea down for the count. In other words, Clapper iced him.

Tiny Thompson, meanwhile, had one of the Quakers leaning over the boards in an extremely uncomfortable position.

Cooney Weiland and Smokey Harris were doing their thing with Shields and Coulson. Seconds later, Shields went at it again with Shore before the peace-loving police and officials could get between them.

The first police on the ice met with immediate resistance and a few misdirected wallops. Soon the reinforcements came, and the fun and games were over.

The penalty box was overcrowded with Owen, Milks, Shore, Shields, Clapper and Coulson. All were assessed majors and fifteen-dollar fines.

A little later, Marty Barry of the Bruins was lugging the puck up ice when, lo and behold, he was sapped by a Quaker named Lowery. It looked like here-we-go-again for a while, but the game ending came shortly after.

Before that, though, Marty Barry, one of the better fighters on the Bruins, was sitting on the bench, fretting about missing the big fight going on out on the ice. Ross finally said to him, "All right, we've won the game, there's only about two minutes to play and you didn't get into the fight. Let's have some more fun. You go out there when the referee drops the puck for the faceoff—and you let the other guy have it. So go ahead, Marty, have your fun."

Out went Barry to take the next faceoff, with malice in his heart. Evidently Gerry Lowery, the Philadelphia center, anticipated what was going to happen because he didn't even wait for the puck to be dropped—he punched Barry right in the mouth before Marty knew what was happening.

Then Silent Night-Star Spangled Banner music was heard while the countdown to the game's end took place.

It was no Christmas for Philadelphia, which has managed only one victory all season. They didn't even win any of the fights on the ice. All in all, the 11,000 fans had a wild and very merry Christmas at the Garden.

This was only the second night that the Bruins didn't sell out the Garden, the other being another holiday, Thanksgiving. If all holidays were like this one, they'd all be sellouts.

Canadiens win playoffs; beat Bruins 3–2 in overtime
LaRochelle scores winning goal for Frenchmen.

This was the series' best clash, filled with excitement, tense moments and bitterness, although after the game Art Ross led his team into the Canadiens' quarters to congratulate the Frenchmen.

Penalties killed the Bruins, as two goals were put across while they were short-handed.

Cooney Weiland put the Bruins back into the game with two third-period tallies. The Forum was jammed to ca-

The famous Dynamite Line—Dit Clapper, Cooney Weiland, Dutch Gainor in 1930.

pacity, and even during the players' warmup organized cheering and singing continued to ring throughout the packed arena. The Forum held only a small percentage of the thousands of fans who anxiously awaited the outcome of the final tilt.

Howie Morenz of Montreal failed to start, so Lepine faced off against Weiland. Lepine was instantly nailed by Hitchman, who in turn was zonked over the skull by Morenz's stick.

The famous Bruins Dynamite Line put strong pressure on goalie Hainsworth. Play zoomed up and down the ice. In the first period Morenz let go from center ice a wicked shot that nearly took Tiny Thompson off his steel runners.

The Bruins suffered a setback when Shore received a penalty for tripping Morenz, who had been hustling all over the place and keeping a powerful barrage on Thompson in the Boston goal.

Owen, battling with Morenz, managed to hit him in the mouth, an action which earned Owen a trip to the cooler with Shore.

Barry, Hitchman and Chapman represented the Bruins on ice. It was one close call after another.

Tiny Thompson spent his time making lightning saves to protect his life. Gagnon let one go from the right wing that Hitch missed with a poke check, and it slipped by Thompson.

Now the enemy was ahead by one.

Owen then tripped Morenz for another penalty, and Lepine got up close for his goal.

The Bruins, as one can tell, had a problem getting the puck out the entire first period.

Shore played this game like a wild elephant with a trunkful of bees. He carried the Boston puck pellmell into anyone in his sight. At times, the Canadiens must have felt that it would have cost a limb to get near him.

Down two goals, the Boston club got one back when Weiland pushed the disc past Hainsworth.

The Rossmen were getting control of their passing, and the Bruins' play in the game was improving.

The Dynamite Line carried the game, and Beattie's Line did the same before Weiland put the rubber on his stick and lifted one over Hainsworth to tie up the contest. Now the score stood Montreal 2, Cooney 2.

In sudden death, the Bruins' strategy was to tire the Montreal Frenchmen, allowing them to carry the fight. The plan went for naught, however, as a rink-wide pass from Marty Burke to LaRochelle was picked up at the right lane just over the line. LaRochelle glided in, took aim and beat Thompson with the victory goal.

The Forum went wild with cheering Frenchmen. The Bruins' dressing room was painted a quiet stone-gray gloom. It would be a long train ride back to the Hub.

March 14, 1933

Hawks forfeit game to Bruins

Coach Gorman attacks referee Stewart. Chicago leaves ice. Police stop near riot.

The 12,000 fans who took in the Bruins-Chicago game at the Garden tonight saw all they could ever expect to see in any hockey game and left without knowing just what the final score was, for referee Bill Stewart, after being pounded badly by Chicago Manager Tommy Gorman, forfeited the contest to the Bruins.

Gorman, with his pearl gray hat, gray coat and pearl gray gloves, had called his players off the ice when the Rossmen were leading 3–2.

It was the first time in memory that a big league hockey team was yanked off the ice by its coach. It is understood that a one-thousand-dollar fine goes with such an act. "But at a time like this, who cares about money?" dapper-dresser Gorman said.

The big jam came after umpire Louis Reycroft had switched on the light for the third Bruins goal in the third minute of the overtime period. The Hawks screamed and kicked, but Reycroft confirmed his decision that the puck was well over the line. The row started when Marty Barry, after taking the shot, was tossed over at the goal mouth onto goalie Gardiner. Other players quickly piled on the squirming mass of bodies around the Chicago net. Coulter of the Hawks assaulted Reycroft by jabbing his stick through the wire. Bill Stewart ordered Coulter off the ice and went over to the Hawk bench to tell Mr. Coulter that he was being invited to depart from the game.

It was then that Gorman whaled Stewart with rights and lefts from his protected spot behind the rail.

Linesman Bill Cleary rushed to stop the melee, and he and Alex Smith held Stewart, who was then livid with rage. Stewart ordered Gorman out, but the order was disregarded until Manager Art Ross crossed the ice to advise Gorman to comply before the Boston police stepped into the picture.

The whole clash was the most fun and games the Garden had seen in some time.

Shore's great efforts had gotten the Bruins clicking on all cylinders, and the big Bruins star came through just two seconds before the regular game ended to tie up the score. Eddie's tally brought on the most colorful demonstration ever witnessed at a Garden game. Hats and paper were tossed on the ice by the gleeful fans.

Shore's goal sent the game into overtime and into the Gorman punching act.

After being ordered off the ice, Gorman walked to the players exit, opened the gate and called his men off the ice.

He yelled to his team captain, Chuck Gardiner, "C'mon off the ice and bring all the guys with you." Gardiner kept shaking his head and saying, "No, no, no."

Gorman insisted so strongly that the Chicago team finally left the ice and followed their angered manager to the dressing room.

Referee Stewart went back to center ice and faced-off the puck without a Hawk in sight. Shore and Chapman faced-off and passed the puck back and forth before Chapman went up to the empty Hawk net and nudged in another Boston goal.

By that time, referee Stewart had skated away and off the ice. It was announced that he had forfeited the game to the Bruins.

The big question remained with the fans: was the final score 1–0, 3–2 or 4–2?

April 3, 1933

Leafs beat Bruins 1–0 after 165 minutes of hard play

The largest crowd ever to see a hockey game in Canada witnessed a new NHL record for a marathon game here in Toronto when the Leafs won a game, 1–0, that took 165 minutes to complete.

The winning goal was poked home by Ken Doraty at 4:46 of the sixth twenty-minute overtime. The old record was 68 minutes extra.

It was a long game, but fortunately none of the players fell asleep.

The end came rather suddenly when Shore, stalling with the puck near his line, lost control for a moment. Blair from Toronto was on it in a leap, and then little Ken Doraty hopped into the play, taking a fast pass and lacing it in past Tiny Thompson.

Around 1 a.m. Ross, noting that his players were dragging their butts, suggested that a coin be tossed to see who would win the long drawn-out game.

Both teams were agreeable, but President Calder thought it would be better if the clubs finished the game without goalies. He figured that at least the goalies could leave and go home to bed.

Tiny made 111 stops for his evening's work. Chabot stopped 89.

Joe Primeau came out of the hospital to play for Toronto, and the Leafs were favored to win by 6–5 odds. Long lines of fans spent the entire day sitting outside the rink, waiting for tickets. They got in, but thousands hung around outside during the game just listening to the noise being generated inside during the 165 minutes of excitement.

Both teams had their bags packed, anticipating the big trip to New York for a final series with the Rangers. Toronto loaded their gear onto a New York train. The Bruins returned their equipment to Boston.

The controversial Conn Smythe, Toronto Maple Leafs owner, relaxing with his spats in a Boston hotel in 1933.

December 12, 1933

Leafs win wild one 4–1

Eddie Shore and Ace Bailey knocked cold. Officials can't handle game.

Two serious injuries came from the wild hockey that took place in Boston Garden between the Maple Leafs and the Bruins. The largest crowd of the year sat in on a 4–1 Toronto victory in the most hatchet-type game to ever be played in Boston.

The game officials were clearly inefficient throughout the entire fracas.

Observers placed the blame for the wild affair squarely on the NHL and on Commissioner of Officials Frank Patrick, who allowed Cleghorn and Daigneault to work this important game after their shameful officiating in the last title series.

In the first period the lax whistle-tooters let the game get out of hand, and finally the players started to take things into their own hands.

The ice battles found Beattie and Clancy, Clapper and Clancy, Cotton, Lamb, and Horner, Gracie and Bailey, and finally Shore and Horner all going hammer and tong at one another.

The Garden ice was soaked with Eddie Shore's blood. He had taken a terrible beating from Toronto sticks while he was guarding the Boston net, trying to aid Tiny Thompson.

A Leaf goal was scored while Shore was being pummeled all over his body. If Shore was unnerved, he could hardly be blamed for his game actions.

The dual cracking of skulls was concentrated into about sixty seconds' time at two isolated places on the Garden ice. The chief participants in the melee besides Ace Bailey were Shore and Red Horner of the Leafs. Horner, a truculent player, is extremely large and well able to take care of himself at all times. He is colorful and capable but has a bad habit of getting into trouble over nothing at all.

The incident started when Eddie Shore carried the puck down ice and was nailed hard against the boards by King Clancy, who spun Shore over his knee and into the back fence. Clancy then grabbed the puck and dashed up ice. Shore, dazed, got slowly to his feet.

The play was down the other end of the ice in Boston territory, and Ace Bailey was skating backwards toward his own blue line. Shore came skating up fast behind Bailey, and they crashed, with Bailey going over Shore. Bailey's head hit the ice with a crack that could be heard all over the Garden. He lay there, his body writhing in convulsive movements as everyone rushed to him.

In the meantime, Shore skated away and was standing near the boards at the blue line when Horner came charging over, enraged at Shore's actions.

Suddenly Horner lashed out with a powerful right hand

that caught Shore flush on the chin, and Shore went down like a log, also hitting his head on the ice.

Eventually the remaining players turned to their injured mates, and both were carried off the ice—Shore to receive medical attention from Dr. Marty Crotty and Bailey from Dr. C. Lynde Gately, the house physician, with Joe Gilmore, manager of the Boston Cubs, assisting.

Ace Bailey, before his injury at Boston Garden.

Shore's head had been cut from the top of the scalp to the nape of the neck. He came to after a few minutes and was revived by the attending doctor.

In the Leaf quarters it was thought at first that Ace Bailey was dead, as all color had left his face and he was beginning to turn blue.

After a hectic and frightening ten minutes, Bailey was brought to in a very dazed condition. He quickly suffered a relapse and was rushed to Audubon Hospital in Boston.

Between periods, Conn Smythe, Leaf owner, got tangled with a Boston fan wearing eyeglasses. The blow that Smythe gave the fan caused a wound requiring three stitches, and glass had to be taken out of his eye. The Bruins fan then prepared to have a warrant issued for Smythe's arrest. As the hostile Boston crowd gathered around the Leaf owner, King Clancy and other players came to his rescue with their sticks.

The high sticks of the Leaf defense were a caution all night for the Bruins to face. The Leafs used basic wood-chopping methods, interference, and board checking, and the two so-called officials didn't do a damned thing about it.

December 13, 1933

Hope fades for Ace Bailey

Stricken player sinks following earlier recovery.

Throughout New England the medical profession is closely following the Bailey case. That he is alive at all is a miracle; the serious hemorrhages should have taken his life quickly. Doctor's attribute Bailey's survival to his great physical constitution and his courage, which have carried him through alternating periods of consciousness and unconsciousness for the past six days.

Dr. Munro managed to stop the bleeding in Bailey's brain, halting the danger at that point.

He is being kept unconscious, although he can be aroused whenever the doctors wish. But if he were to become conscious, it would cause him fatigue that might snuff out his life.

No blood transfusions are possible, since they, like other nourishment, would overload the blood circulation and be fatal.

Bailey is being fed intravenously, and carbon dioxide and oxygen inhalations are also being used.

The medical staff at City Hospital are amazed that Bailey is still alive. As one of the attending people remarked, "We have rummies [drunks] brought here with fewer complications, and they are dead in twelve hours."

Bailey is not a drinking man. He is well conditioned and at the time of his injury was in perfect physical shape.

Meanwhile, Eddie Shore has been on raw edge as the result of serious nervous strain. Each day has been increasingly difficult, and friends have said they never believed he could become so emotional.

Shore keeps in constant touch with Bailey's condition at City Hospital. All the Bruins, for that matter, are concerned over the incident, and they are attempting to aid in any way they can.

Manager Art Ross has offered Mrs. Bailey the use of his car as long as she stays in Boston.

Last night President Adams announced that the total proceeds from an upcoming game between the Bruins and Montreal will be turned over to Mrs. Bailey.

It was also announced at a second press conference that Babe Siebert has been obtained from the New York Rangers for Vic Ripley and Roy Burmeister, who had been a Boston Cubs holdout. Myles Lane of Melrose is now programmed as a reserve defense man for the Bruins. Bert McInenly has been signed to help out on defense, since Eddie Shore will be out of action until the Bailey situation is resolved.

December 19, 1933

Bruins whip Maroons in overtime 1–0 on lucky Gracie goal

Mrs. Ace Bailey receives $6,643.22 gate receipts.

While Ace Bailey was still making a valiant battle for existence at Boston City Hospital, it was the same old story at Boston Garden: the show must go on.

A lucky shot by Bob Gracie, who flung a feed from far up the left boards to Oliver, caromed off Cy Wentworth's stick past goalie Andy Kerr for a tally. It all happened at 6:24 of overtime.

The Bruins and the Garden had put on the game to assist Mrs. Ace Bailey. A Boston crowd of about 6,500 paid a total of $6,643.22, and this amount was turned over to the injured Toronto player's wife.

It was the second smallest attendance of the year. Looking at the empty seats, one of the players felt it was because the second to the bottom Maroon team was playing, but one member of the press thought that Bailey's injury had turned the minds of the Bruins' followers from pro hockey.

Halfway through the game, a tremendous cheer went up when it was announced that Ace Bailey's condition had changed from poor to fair.

The first period hadn't gone ten minutes before some in the audience started to yell, "We want Shore," and more and more of the fans took up the cry, many others applauding the generous gesture.

Melrose's Myles Lane, up from the Cubs, was wearing

Shore's number 2 jersey, and he got a hand when he glided out to relieve Dit Clapper, who had started the game in Shore's slot.

Lionel Hitchman was the number-one star in the contest. As usual his work featured some outstanding hockey, with his rushes, passes and vital stick interceptions. While Hitchman spent the night mostly on offense, Perk Galbraith came through with some fantastic defensive maneuvers as he broke up many of the Maroons' return thrusts.

Early hockey-helmet art.

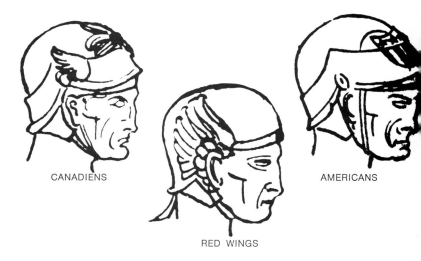

CANADIENS

RED WINGS

AMERICANS

BRUINS

RANGERS

December 27, 1933

Boston architect designs artistic, symbolic helmets

One of Boston's leading architects, who happens to be a hockey fan but prefers anonymity, has come up with some interesting helmet creations. Being an architect, he is greatly influenced by symbolism; thus, he was instantly seized with the thought that hockey players should borrow ideas from old-timers and go in for symbolic headgear. The helmets are designed to protect the players and also to delight the artistic soul.

The Bruins will have a bear's head on the helmet. The New York Rangers' helmets will carry a steer. The Canadiens will wear the fleur-de-lis in front, with wings on the sides. Toronto, of course, will wear a maple leaf. The Ottawa Senators will feature an official-looking crown and other appurtenances. The New York Americans will appear with an American shield. The Red Wings from Detroit will carry wing engravings, while the Chicago Blackhawks will also have wings to go with a hawk's head in front.

The Montreal Maroons will have to figure out an insignia or else change their nickname, but that's their problem.

It is said that the idea could be carried even further. The NHL teams could change their names to Latin. So, the Boston Bruins would become Ursi Bostoniae.

14,500 pay $17,000 to Ace Bailey
Game wide open as Leafs defeat All-Stars 7–3.

A full house in Toronto contributed $17,000 to Ace Bailey, the badly injured Leaf player.

An All-Star aggregation composed of top NHL personalities was on the short end of the hockey stick by a score of 7–3.

Eddie Shore received a rink-shattering ovation when he received from Ace Bailey's hand the commemorative medal presented by Leo Dandurand of the Montreal Canadiens.

The All-Star lineup included Gardiner (Chicago) in goal, Ching Johnson (Rangers) and Shore (Boston) on defense, Morenz (Canadiens) at center, W. Cook (Rangers) at right wing, and Joliat (Canadiens) at left wing.

December 1934

Modified football helmet designed by Art Ross protects head against injury

Art Ross, manager of the Boston Bruins, has designed a hockey helmet. The headpiece is designed to guard the player against injuries such as the one suffered by Ace Bailey.

Unlike the boxing-protector style or the rugby type put forth by Jack Adams of Detroit, Ross's helmet has no ear pieces, and the top is constructed of leather straps instead of solid leather. There are eight straps on the top. The protection comes from sponge rubber next to the leather, and felt covers the inside of the rubber. The front has about a two-inch width to cover the forehead, and the back is about four inches wide.

The straps on top offer protection against high sticks, a safeguard that other helmets don't have.

Art Chapman of the Bruins was one of the first players to try one on, and he gave it his instant approval. However, he refused to let anyone try a high stick on his head, even as a test.

December 1934

Shore leaves town

Eddie Shore left Boston today, departing quietly for an undisclosed destination. It is not believed that he has gone to Florida, Bermuda or Cuba, since he took his skates with him.

The Edmonton Express, Eddie Shore.

December 8, 1935

Bruins win 3–1
Clapper stars. Dit scores two.

Boston fans have not lost faith in the Bruins, even after their recent 6–0 defeat at the hands of the Chicago Blackhawks. The faithful swarmed back to the Garden to bulge the place into a new season attendance mark of 15,000.

People were glad they went to see a perfect Bruins team sweep by the dynamic Toronto Maple Leafs in a way that brought renewed interest in the Bruins' chances of climbing to the top.

Beating the Leafs was a stunt of strength. The Toronto team has been defeated only five times this season.

All night long, King Clancy and Red Horner, Toronto's two rascals, handed out board checks that went unnoticed, except by the Boston fans, one of whom got so burned up that he scaled his new derby at Clancy, who golfed it back over the boards in a badly battered condition. It was clearly shown that Clancy can do a job on a derby as well as on a puck.

Dit Clapper.

December 29, 1935

Tiny Thompson blanks Americans 4–0

Bruins' star goalie has sensational game. Six former Bruins play for Amerks.

Apparently disgusted at the spectacular saves made by the little wonder goalie Roy Worters in past New York-Boston games, Tiny Thompson gave one of the Garden's finest exhibitions of the year when he shut out the Americans.

Of interest was the fact that the New York club had six ex-Bruins in its lineup.

Former Bean Towners were Harry Oliver, who played right wing for eight years in Boston before being traded last summer, Art Chapman, Alex Smith, Happy Emms, Lloyd Klein and Eddie Burke.

One of the present Bruins remarked after the game, "It's a good thing there's a Bruins or perhaps there wouldn't be an Americans."

December 13, 1936

Bruins push by Amerks 4–3

Boston flies to early lead. Youngster Milton Schmidt plays first Bruins game.

The Boston Bruins held on to third place in the United States section of the NHL by defeating the Americans 4–3 in a rough, exciting match before 12,000 New York fans.

The Bruins flashed fast and smooth combination plays behind a stout defense, tearing into the Amerks from the outset and grabbing a three-goal lead in the first thirty-seven minutes of play. Red Beattie, Bunny Cook, with his first marker of the season, and Nels Stewart scored, in that order. Getliffe got the final goal in the third period.

Twelve penalties were handed out during the hectic fray, the Bruins getting eight, including one ten-minute misconduct to new Bruin Milton Schmidt for fighting with Eddie Wiseman in the third period.

Young Schmidt was recently called up from Providence. He caught the Boston-to-New York train and traveled with the Bruins to Gotham City.

December 1936

Bruins help put Garden in black for first time in eight years

For the first time in its eight years of existence, the Boston Garden, at a meeting of the board of directors, declared a dividend of three dollars per share on preferred stock. Bigger crowds and more money for sporting events were credited with the surplus the North Station made in the recently closed fiscal year.

After losing money steadily for the first six years after its opening on November 18, 1928, the Garden finally had a good year. All connections with the Madison Square Garden Corporation have been dissolved.

George V. Brown, manager of the Arena for many years, became general manager of the Garden and Arena Corporation two years ago. Since that time, the corporation as a whole has been making money.

The profit, the amount of which the board did not disclose, is a result of the steady attendance at all Bruins games, the success of a winter carnival and a rodeo, and the revived interest in wrestling caused by Danno O'Mahoney's winning the heavyweight title.

❖❖❖❖❖❖

January 19, 1937 . . . . . Weston Adams and Conn Smythe wear tails to game.

There is a story told about a Major McLaughlin from Chicago, who became upset about the lack of dignity in NHL hockey.

McLaughlin's wife was Irene Castle, of the famous dance team of Vernon and Irene Castle. Soon after their marriage, Mrs. McLaughlin started designing hockey uniforms and kept pressing the idea that people should dress better at hockey games.

Echoing his wife's statements, Major McLaughlin talked to sports writers about his wife's thoughts.

One night, as a gag, Weston Adams and Conn Smythe dressed up in tails for a Boston-Toronto game at the Garden.

Evidently the full dress for a Bruins game didn't catch on, because it lasted only one night. Too bad it didn't pan out, because it would have looked nice to see all the gang in the second balcony decked out in full bloom.

❖❖❖❖❖❖

Art Ross and Conn Smythe feud.

They were a couple of fierce competitors, always trying to get the edge on each other. They fought over players, games, remarks and everything imaginable.

One night in Boston at a Bruins-Toronto game, Art Ross was suffering with a touch of diverticulitis—in other words, a sore end.

Just to give poor Ross the needle, Smythe ordered some roses from a Boston florist and had them delivered to the Leaf bench. Then he sent King Clancy skating to the Bruins' bench with the flowers.

Clancy said to Ross, "Art, these are for you, from Conn."

Clancy skated off, saying to Ross, "Conn says to be sure and read the card."

The Boston manager opened the envelope, read the card and flung the flowers on the seats behind the bench.

The card from Smythe had said, "Dear Art—Take these flowers and stick 'em up your ass."

Ross was really sore, and not just in the rear end, either.

◆◆◆◆◆◆◆

Ace Bailey and King Clancy, Toronto Maple Leafs, sitting in stands after Bailey's recovery from his near-fatal accident in 1933.

Opposite:
Cooney Weiland and Milt Schmidt.

March 10, 1937

Garden fans express grief over Morenz's death

Pay wonderful tribute at Garden.

In a darkened Boston Garden that had once known the magic of his flashing skates and the rifling speed of his shot, Howie Morenz, who died late Monday night, was solemnly honored by 13,000 fans as the Bruins and the Detroit Red Wings said their final goodbyes to the greatest center hockey has ever known.

It was an impressive sight as a thin moving spotlight illuminated the faceoff circle where two tattered gloves, a stick and a puck lay.

The rest of the Garden was pitch black. Across each blue line stood the Bruins and the Red Wings at strict attention. It was one of those quiet moments a sports arena knows once in a lifetime.

The second-balcony hockey fans, who call themselves the "130" Club because they sit in section 130, took up a collection and gave it to Art Ross to buy flowers for Morenz, who was their idol. The collection totaled thirteen dollars and twelve cents, and Ross added another five dollars.

Howie Morenz has died, but he surely is not forgotten in Boston.

The Bruins gave the fans a preview of their Stanley Cup playoff plans by storming all over Detroit and coming out with a 6–1 win. Dit Clapper was the game's high scorer.

March 24, 1937

Bruins lose to Montreal Maroons 4–1

Opening playoff game baffles B's. Dit Clapper swings at referee.

The Bruins arrived in Montreal with a fourteen-man team, one less than the player limit. A throat ailment to Bun Cook, veteran winger, reduced the Bruins' strength.

Boston figured it could win this series if their defense of Jack Portland, Allan Shields, Flash Hollett and Hooley Smith could keep the Maroons from shooting fifteen feet in front of Tiny Thompson, the net minder.

The Maroons, riding herd on their late-year winning streak into the Stanley Cup playoffs, wore down the powerful Bruins and stung the United States section second placers 4–1 in the opening game of the best-of-three playoffs. Getliffe got the only Bruins score in the third period, assisted by Cowley and Sands.

There are only two players in the NHL whom Dit Clapper has problems with: Dave Trottier of the Maroons and Art Coulter of the Rangers.

Trottier bothered Dit because Clapper thought the Mon-

treal player was a little on the dirty side. One time, near the end of the game, Trottier gave Clapper the stick. Dit stopped and knocked Trottier down with one punch and started pounding the hell out of him on the ice. Clarence Campbell, the referee, came over to Clapper and said, "Clapper, you're a yellow ———— to be hitting a man when he's down." Clapper was so outraged that he turned around and belted Campbell.

Tommy Gorman, Maroons coach, wanted Clapper suspended for the rest of the playoffs.

Later, standing around in the Windsor Hotel lobby in Montreal, Art Ross and Clapper were waiting for a call from Frank Calder, NHL president, to see what would happen to Clapper for hitting the referee.

Ross finally got the call from Calder and hurried back to Dit with the message. "It's all taken care of. You're not being bounced out of the series. It's just a fine."

Clarence Campbell had contacted Calder and admitted that it was his fault and not Clapper's. He said that he should not have sworn at Dit. Campbell was a real man to admit his fault and clear the player of blame.

October 28, 1937

Walter Brown fills father's spot

Named new head of Garden-Arena.

At a special meeting of the board of directors of the Boston Garden-Arena Corporation yesterday, Walter A. Brown was unanimously elected general manager of the Boston Garden and Boston Arena. Brown succeeds his father, the late George V. Brown.

In taking over the reins of New England's great sports enterprise, Walter Brown will be the youngest man ever to hold that office. He is only thirty-two years of age.

Walter A. Brown, Hockey Hall of Fame member.

October 1937 . . . . . The Kraut Line.

The Kraut Line was actually put together when they were just kids. Boyhood chums, they played at Providence, and the nickname came from Albert LeDuc, who coached them in Rhode Island. They were from German families, so naturally the name Krauts applied. It was later changed to the Kitchener Kids because of the harsh feelings toward the Germans during World War II.

The first two to come up to the Bruins were Milt Schmidt and Woody Dumart, who joined the team for the 1936–37 season. Their first right winger was Dit Clapper.

Art Ross advised Clapper, "Take care of the kids out there on the ice until they get the feel of things."

Clapper did as Ross commanded until they proved they could more than hold their own in the NHL.

Schmidt and Dumart were up for about a half-season before Bobby Bauer was given the big call.

It was one of the greatest lines in NHL history, and if Bauer hadn't had a problem with his heart they might have played a lot longer and made many more records. As it was, they missed three years during World War II service.

Bauer was the oldest, and it was he and Dumart who first told Schmidt about the Bruins.

Art Ross wrote to Schmidt, "I'd like to have you come to our training camp next year for a tryout."

Milt replied, "I'll start saving right now." Milt was going to save up for expenses to get to camp, not knowing that the Bruins would cover everything.

He reported and received a pair of skates, the first new pair he had ever owned.

◆◆◆◆◆◆◆

Bruins' super Kraut Line—Bobby Bauer, Milt Schmidt, Woody Dumart.

November 6, 1937

Bruins open new season, win 4–2

Ray Getliffe gets three goals in Montreal duel.

This was a bristling opener that featured Getliffe's hat trick. The blond Boston wingman carried his team from behind in the first period to a 2–1 advantage, and his third goal raised that to 3–1.

Young Milt Schmidt, who is constantly improving, came through with the fourth Bruins tally.

The game was marked by mid-season speed and heavy hitting, although it was only the first contest of the season.

King Clancy's baptism as Maroons coach was a disappointment to the big opening-night crowd, but Clancy iced a team that refused to let down. Included in his lineup was Des Smith, brought up from Ottawa amateur ranks less than twenty-four hours before the game to play on defense.

The redoubtable Eddie Shore, out most of last season with a back injury, led many charges up the ice for the B's. It looks as if the Bruins' great star will be as good as ever in 1937–1938.

The Babe Ruth of the NHL, Eddie Shore.

November 14, 1937

Bruins open at Garden tonight

Shore on comeback trail.

A potentially powerful Bruins club will skate out on the Garden ice tonight against the Rangers from New York. Superbly conditioned after a month of pre-season training and rated by experts as the best Boston team in years, the Bruins are confident they will fulfill all pre-season predictions.

In many ways, this promises to be an unusual Boston opener. Hopes of the fans are high. The Bruins promise to be a lot faster, better balanced, and higher scoring than anything Boston has cheered in years.

Hockey's greatest player, Eddie Shore, is making an amazing comeback that Bruins players say will once again carry him right to the top.

Montreal fans booed Shore as they haven't booed him in years for his aggressive play against the Maroons in the Bruins' first game. Standing on their feet, they hooted him as he foiled Maroon drives time after time with his outstanding play. Boston fans will have as much interest in what Shore shows tonight as in any other part of the hockey opener.

The fans have another great year of thrills in store if the "Babe Ruth of hockey," Eddie Shore, is really as good as ever.

This is, however, in no way a one-man Bruins team. Shore only tops what is otherwise, in the opinion of President Adams and Art Ross, the finest hockey team that has ever worn the Bruins' colors.

It is also the youngest team ever, with Getliffe, Cowley, Schmidt, Dumart, Bauer, Jackson and Portland among the youngest men playing in the NHL.

Recent Bruins practice sessions at the Arena have been outstanding, with all the players working their tails off.

Dit Clapper has for the first time been playing back on defense, which should give the fans plenty to talk about.

November 14, 1937

Bruins flash to top over Rangers 3–2
15,000 welcome Bruins at Garden.

Once again big-time hockey has come into its own for another new season, and 15,000 whooped it up when the Bruins won the opening game.

Bauer, Schmidt and Cowley accounted for the Bruins' scores. Bobby Bauer was first to sock home a bulb-lighting shot, getting off a back-hander in the first minutes of play, while Art Coulter was serving time for being a bad guy.

With the Bruins short-handed in the second period, Milt Schmidt broke down his end, with only Dave Kerr to beat in the Rangers net, and put one home to give Boston two goals.

In the second stanza, Bill Cowley, using Ray Getliffe as a decoy, jammed home the clincher.

◆◆◆◆◆◆◆

Shore's Skates.

Number 2 was a fussy guy about his skates.

One night before a Bruins' game at the Garden, he came charging at Win Green, the Bruins' trainer. "Hey, look at these bleeping blades! They're dull as hell. Get 'em sharpened, I can't play on these."

Green took the skates, yelled to his assistant, Walter Randall, and with a big wink said, "Randall, go jump a cab and take these over to the Arena and get 'em sharpened for Eddie."

Randall took off like a bullet, running down the ramp into North Station, where he rushed up to one of the seats in the railroad waiting room. He sat down, picked up a newspaper and read the sports pages for about fifteen minutes.

Then he flung down the paper, dashed back up the Garden ramp into the Bruins' dressing room, where Shore was impatiently waiting for his skates' return.

Shore held the blades up to his eye and murmured, "Now, that's much better. That's how my skates should be sharpened all the time."

And with that, Shore skated out on the Garden ice and played his usual spectacular game, thanks to the Green-Randall skate-sharpening method.

◆◆◆◆◆◆◆

Three old Bruins pros talking shop with Art Ross.
Left to right: Cooney Weiland, Dit Clapper and Eddie Shore.

Eddie Shore back in lineup

Starts thirteenth year.

The NHL's renowned Eddie Shore will make his thirteenth annual ice debut to hockey fans at Boston Garden tonight against the Red Wings from Detroit.

Shore, who just left the list of player holdouts four days ago, has kept in top condition by working out with his Bruins teammates.

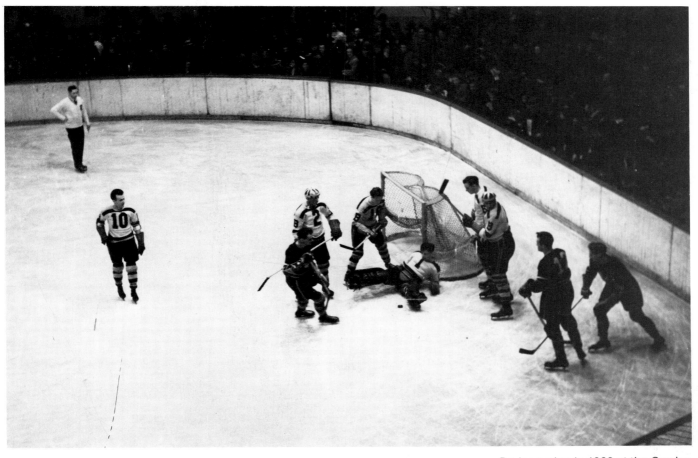

Bruins action in 1938 at the Garden.

◆◆◆◆◆◆

September 1938 . . . . . Ross calls press conference. Hurricane comes same day.

In September 1938 Art Ross called a press conference on the same day of the famous hurricane. That was also the day the old Boston Braves were playing at Braves Field. One of the ball players hit a pop fly that was going back into the grandstand. It never got there but landed near second base as powerful winds started to whip around the ball field.

Beans Reardon, the umpire, watched the ball land behind second base and yelled to the players, "I don't know what the hell is going on, but this game is called as of now."

Through the hurricane and all, the press managed to arrive at Ross's conference.

Art Ross asked the press members there, "What do

you think about replacing Tiny Thompson with Frankie Brimsek?"

Thompson was a big favorite with the local papers, and they told Ross, "Don't do it."

At the Bruins' break-up party the previous season, Thompson had stood up and made a short speech. "We played great hockey, but we didn't play winning hockey." Tiny had clearly become disenchanted with the Bruins' wide-open style of play, and he made no effort to hide his feelings.

Thompson's statement had been on Ross's mind for some time; it was one of the major things that forced the issue of Thompson's trade. The Bruins started the 1938 year with Tiny in the nets, but that didn't last too long.

◆◆◆◆◆◆

November 29, 1938

Fans upset over Thompson trade
Clapper blasts deal that ends Tiny's eleven-year reign in Bruins net.

Tiny Thompson traded to Detroit! Those were the words all Boston heard.

Tiny's close buddy and roommate Dit Clapper blew his top and roared, "They can trade me too. First they took Marty Barry, and now it's Tiny. I don't want to stay here while my best friends are with the Red Wings."

Art Ross finally sat the big defense man down and cooled him off after a lengthy coach-to-player chat.

"I guess I put the Bruins in a tough spot," Clapper said. "We'd better forget it. Besides, Ross said he wouldn't trade me, anyhow."

Clapper and Thompson have been close friends since they joined the team eleven years ago. So it was no wonder Dit saw red.

Four-time winner of the George Vezina Trophy for the most valuable goal tender in the NHL, Thompson had been a big man on many Bruins teams. His reckless, daring hockey skill, the fact that he loved every minute of ice action, and the fact that he had dragged his sick body out of bed many times to fill the gap in the Bruins net—this is now all gone.

Ross admitted, "Thompson is a fine goal tender, but there are several good reasons why we traded him to Detroit.

"We are confident that Brimsek is just as good as Thompson, and we need the money from the trade to develop more young players. Finally, we think this is an excellent time to settle a problem which has troubled all of us, including Thompson, since the beginning of the season."

To those close to the situation, the Thompson trade was no real surprise. "It's been coming to a head for some time," said one observer.

The matter of salary was part of the delicate situation. Tiny felt he deserved more money than he was getting.

Back in 1932, when the Bruins brought up the two rookie goalies Percy Jackson and Wilf Cude, Thompson left the squad for a short time, and the Bruins stated he had gone away to rest to avoid a "nervous breakdown."

Thompson resented the wording of the Bruins' statement, and from that time on his relations with the club were strained.

The two rookies didn't cut the mustard and were released, leaving Thompson as the lone goal tender.

When he reported for the 1938 season, he realized he couldn't play effectively for the Bruins under these tense conditions. He insisted on a two-year clause in his contract and requested that he be traded to Detroit if possible.

Detroit beckoned, and Tiny Thompson left.

The Krauts in 1938 action.

Mr. Zero, Frank Brimsek, 1938–39—1942–43; 1945–46—1948–49. Hockey Hall of Fame, and another great career interrupted by World War II.

November 30, 1938

Thompson bids Boston farewell
Brimsek arrives to replace Tiny.

Tiny Thompson moves on now to his next net-minding location, Detroit. Boston fans haven't received such a shock since Babe Ruth was sold to the New York Yankees.

Tiny always did his part in front of the Bruins' gas pipes and made a favorable impression on Bostonians during his eleven years in the Hub. He might have stayed in Boston for some time to come, yet it seems fitting that he is passing out of the local picture while he's still the league's best goal tender.

Old Number 1 showed up at practice yesterday to say goodbye to his buddies. It was rather a sad parting as he lugged his gear out of the Boston dressing room for the last time in his career.

Frank Brimsek, Tiny's successor, is due in from Providence tonight or early tomorrow.

Rest of 1938 season . . . . . Art Ross is right about Brimsek.

Art Ross had great faith in the young Brimsek, who was twenty-two when he was called up to replace Tiny Thompson. Ross felt extremely confident that before too long the Bruins' fans would be raving about the new man in the nets.

The Bruins' manager had been planning for the future success of the B's and knew that Brimsek would come through.

Brimsek arrived in Boston and lost his first game, but then came the good things.

Twice during the 1938–1939 season Frank Brimsek chalked up three consecutive shutouts. He also set a record by playing 231 minutes and 54 seconds without allowing a goal. These feats quickly earned him the nickname "Mr. Zero."

Ross was right again. Brimsek was good, damned good.

◆◆◆◆◆◆◆

April 1, 1939

Rangers win 3–1, even series
Two goals in last period beat Bruins.

Just when the Bruins were hoping to bag Game Six of the NHL championship series and walk off with the Stanley Cup, Les Patrick's Rangers April-fooled the Rossmen, taking advantage of two consecutive penalties to break a 1–1 deadlock. The Rangers forged ahead to a 3–1 victory.

Mel Hill scored the lone goal for the Bruins.

April 2, 1939

Manager's berth due Shore

It was reported that Eddie Shore would make an announcement that he may become a minor league hockey manager before the start of next season.

The biggest ice star the Bruins have ever had is seriously considering retirement from active playing at the end of the current season.

He once figured that he was a contender for the managerial job with the Bruins, but he felt he would have a better future if he got a short training period in the International circuit.

April 4, 1939

Hill hero again as Bruins win 2–1
Rookie scores big goal in third overtime at Garden against Rangers.

At 12:35 in the third overtime period, Mel Hill became the hero of the series. He had taken Cowley's passes twice before to win games in this never-ending Stanley Cup series.

Roy Conacher started the play, and Bill Cowley picked it up in the right corner and fed back toward center, where Hill shoveled up the puck, took one stride and fired in the deciding goal.

The Bruins and the Rangers each scored once in the second period. The Bruins' Ray Getliffe angled in Pettinger's thirty-five-footer for the first tally, and Muzz Patrick of the Rangers followed three minutes later with the tying goal.

Frank Ryan made an appeal over the loudspeakers, asking the fans not to throw objects on the ice as spectators had done during the previous game. Two fans didn't get the word and were arrested, one for throwing a bottle, the other for tossing a potato.

Another near fight cropped up between Clapper and Art Coulter, who don't seem to be the best of friends. Ross ordered Dit off the ice before he could prolong the heated discussion with Coulter.

Both teams started jamming around the pair, and for a while it looked like a repeat of the great New York fight of before. Cooler heads prevailed, though, and things quieted down.

The sixty-minute bell sounded shortly after, and the clubs left the ice for a ten-minute rest period before the overtime, the fourth time in the series an extra period has been required.

The overtime period wore on, with the Bruins holding the advantage in everything except the score until Hill took over.

Bobby Bauer scores one for the Bruins.

*Bruins and Rangers tangle
one more time in 1939.*

Weiland, Shore and Clapper outside Bruins' dressing room after 1939 game in Boston. Smiles tell the story: they must have won.

April 6, 1939

Bruins stomp Leafs 2–1

Bauer's solo dash breaks open tame game.

This was a quiet kind of a playoff game. The Bruins' play was way off, and this was proved in the second period when they didn't even take a shot on Turk Broda in the Leaf net that could be listed as a save. As far as can be recalled, that has never before happened to any Bruins team.

The ice might have had something to do with the Bruins' play, for the surface wasn't as fast as usual. The Garden was unable to turn on the air drafts because of the heavy rain in Boston.

The game dragged badly at times, and the Boston Gallery Gods fumed and hooted, showing their displeasure. Many of those among the Gallery Gods were frisked be-fore being allowed to the second tier. Some of the "give ups" were odd enough. Three fans had part of a quart, and they were instructed to either finish it or leave it, as all bottles were barred. They happily finished it. Others had bottled beer, and they were told to "drink up or throw away." In general, the night's take was hardly up to expectations. But bottle precautions were necessary owing to the barrages at previous games.

Bobby Bauer became the hero when he started a solo near his own line, raced down the right lane, swerved around the Leaf defense and went up to within three feet of Broda before sending home the winning tally.

1939 ice action against the Toronto Maple Leafs.

Eddie Shore pulling off his working clothes after another hard night's work.

Eddie Shore points up ice to his son in the 1930s.

Preceding page: *1938–39 Stanley Cup champions.*
Front row—Roy Conacher, Mel Hill, Charlie Sands,
Cooney Weiland, Milt Schmidt, Gordon Pettinger,
Flash Hollett
Back row—Frank Brimsek, John Crawford, Eddie Shore,
Woody Dumart, Bobby Bauer, Dit Clapper, Bill Cowley,
Jack Portland, Ray Getliffe

◆◆◆◆◆◆◆

Shore bridges Brydges.

One thing for sure—Eddie Shore never ducked trouble.

In playing against the New York Americans, the Bruins faced a certain young man named Billy Brydges, who played back on defense. He had been trouble for Eddie earlier in the game, as he had flattened Number 2 not once but three times in the contest. One check was so violent that Shore lay on the ice for a few minutes. Twice Shore had to be assisted off, but he returned each time, to the cheers of the crowd.

Late in the game, Shore came down the ice once again, and once again Mr. Brydges got set to hit Eddie. But this time the Boston star was ready. Brydges came steaming right into the butt end of Shore's stick.

The few teeth that Mr. Brydges had were no longer, for they now lay on the ice.

Eddie Shore played not only an eye for an eye but a tooth for a tooth.

The New York Americans player was last seen consulting with a dentist in the dressing room.

◆◆◆◆◆◆◆

April 1939

Eddie Shore's last rush up ice

The cruel hand of time, being what it is, has started to draw down the curtain on another great career.

Sports people, former players, and hockey fans everywhere are commencing to discuss how much longer the great Eddie Shore can last. The human body can stand only so much.

Eddie is not too old in years, but in one sense—the physical sense—he is definitely nearing the end of the line.

His legs have slowed, but, like other athletes, he has learned to use his head more when the rest of his body does not respond. He has reached the peak of mental stardom.

Number 2 was a super-great hockey player back in his halcyon days, when he would come steaming down the ice, knocking whole teams ass over tea kettles and blasting away with his powerful shot. Eddie Shore was a spectacular performer, and the crowd flew out of their seats with a roar every time he took off with the puck.

Shore has been not only the best of the Bruins but the best player in hockey.

The one guy Shore can't lick is age. We all grow old. So will Eddie Shore, and one day he'll take his last rush up ice.

Opposite: *The Krauts, also known as the Kitchener Kids.*

The War Years

Shore dons helmet for another hectic Bruins battle.

January 11, 1940

Ross not selling Shore to Americans

Art Ross answered a question in the Garden lobby. "We are not thinking of selling Eddie Shore to the New York Americans."

Right now Shore isn't much use to the Bruins or to any other club in the NHL, for he hasn't been around to make his drawing power felt at home or on the road.

Shore has been sitting by and watching the progress of the Springfield Indians hockey club, which he recently purchased.

The famous Number 2 has meant a lot to the Boston Bruins and their fans. Through the years he has become the NHL's Mr. Hockey. Shore has been paid well by the Bruins for his services; as far as salary goes, Shore cannot hope to get more with the New York Americans than he has been offered by the Bruins. With the Hub club he would get $300 for each regular-season home game and $300 for each home playoff game, which in the long run would amount to something like $8,000, which would exceed the league salary limit of $7,500 per year.

It seems to be a Mexican standoff between Eddie Shore and the Bruins hockey team.

Number 2 starting one of his well-known dashes up ice.

Shore traded to Americans

Bruins get Eddie Wiseman. Deal okay with Edmonton Eddie.

The Boston Bruins have finally ended their dealings with Eddie Shore.

Shore and Manager Art Ross have been at odds since Shore purchased the Springfield team in the International American League.

It was announced today by the Bruins that "the Edmonton Express" has been traded to the New York Americans for Eddie Wiseman, veteran right winger.

The trade gets Ross and the Bruins off the hook and at the same time gives Shore, who has played a fourteen-year career with the Bruins, a free hand to do what he wants for himself and his new Springfield team.

According to Shore, his arrangement with Red Dutton, part-owner and manager of the Americans, permits him to skate for the Indians whenever he deems it necessary, at home or on the road, and calls for his physical appearance in a certain number of games for the Amerks in New York and on the road.

"Dutton is allowing me to do just what Ross wouldn't," said Shore. "Where the Bruins couldn't see fit to let me play anywhere but in Springfield or Boston, Dutton is perfectly willing to let me play wherever I care to in this league, as long as I live up to my agreement to play the required number of games in New York."

Shore continued, "Since I have spent my entire career in Boston, and since Boston fans have always given me grand treatment, I hate to leave this city, but the situation with the Bruins was getting worse instead of better, and I feel very well satisfied with the arrangement as it stands now."

In a statement announcing the big trade, Art Ross said, "Convinced that Eddie Shore was no longer interested in playing hockey in Boston, the Bruins acceded to his final wish that he become associated with the New York Americans. That desire was communicated to me by Manager Dutton, and, after discussion by telephone with President Weston Adams, the Bruins agreed to make a trade with the Americans for Wiseman, if satisfactory to Shore."

In a wire to Ross, Shore stated, "Deal with Americans is satisfactory to me."

Shore leaves. Wiseman comes. The Bruins continue on.

Eddie Wiseman, 1939–40—1941–42, came to the Bruins from the New York Americans in the Eddie Shore trade.

Early shot of Dit Clapper, with helmet.

Schmidt and Clapper chosen for All-Star team

Milt Schmidt, Boston's veteran Kraut Line center, and Dit Clapper, a big cog on defense, were the Bruins selected to the All-Star team this year.

Clapper was a member of the 1939 group. This is the first time around for Milton Conrad Schmidt.

Eddie Shore, traded to the New York Americans in mid-season by Boston, was passed over for only the second time in the years the teams have been picked.

Milt Schmidt.

The Krauts—Bauer, Schmidt, Dumart.

1940 playoffs.

The Krauts finished one-two-three in scoring during the 1939–40 season. It was a better Bruins team than the one that took the Cup in 1939. However, the Cup didn't remain in Boston that year—the Bruins lost to the Rangers on account of injuries to several key players.

◆◆◆◆◆◆◆

Bruins player down and out in a 1940 game.

March 19, 1941

Bruins on Top, 4–1

Rossmen keep Mowers from Vezina. Final game of season.

The 1940–41 season finished last night for the Bruins at Boston Garden, where they helped Turk Broda of the Maple Leafs to the Vezina Trophy without Broda's even making a save.

The burly Leaf net minder, watching the final game of the year from a box seat, was a goal away from Johnny Mowers of Detroit when the game started.

It took the Bruins only fifty-four seconds to break the twenty-four-year-old heart of rookie goalie Johnny Mowers, who, with only ninety-eight goals scored against him for the year, was one up on Broda for the big award.

Bill Cowley got credit for the goal that went by Mowers and caused the Red Wing to lose the Vezina Trophy.

The Bruins finished the year in first place in the NHL, with twenty-seven wins, eight losses, and thirteen ties, for a total of sixty-seven points. They scored 168 goals and allowed opponents to score 102 times.

April 12, 1941

Bruins take Stanley Cup finale 3–1

Four straight over Detroit. New series record.

The hard-skating Boston Bruins tonight set a new Stanley Cup playoff record by shooting down the Detroit team 3–1 to carry off hockey's highest honors.

They won in four straight games, an accomplishment unprecedented in the NHL.

Frankie Brimsek was outstanding and put on a terrific display of goal tending.

Nick Damore, 1941–42.

The Bruins had to come from behind to overhaul Detroit and bring the Stanley Cup back to Bean Town.

One of the smallest Stanley Cup crowds in history, 8,125, sat in on the series finale at Detroit.

It was the second time in three years that the Bruins have won the world championship and it was the first time that a four-out-of-seven final series has been completed in four games.

Immediately following the game, the Bruins departed by train for Boston.

When the game ended, both teams went to center ice to shake hands. President Weston Adams, Art Ross, Jack Adams and President Frank Calder grouped with the players for the Cup presentation.

Flash Hollett and Bobby Bauer scored second-period goals. Eddie Wiseman tallied in the third stanza.

Right now the Cup is riding on the train back to Boston. Keep it shiny, boys!

Cooney Weiland, Art Ross and Weston Adams proudly displaying the Prince of Wales Trophy.

69

December 7, 1941 . . . . . Where were you on Pearl Harbor Day?

On Pearl Harbor Day the Bruins were playing in New York, where they were nosed out 5–4 by the Rangers. The Boston defense fell apart in the second period, and the Bruins' string of six straight wins was ended.

Milt Schmidt got the first goal almost immediately after the puck was dropped.

He slammed a vicious low shot that sped hard into the corner of the net. Henry, the Rangers' goal tender, had his eye on Woody Dumart and saw Schmidt's shot too late to cover it. Other Boston scorers on that memorable night were Dumart, Herb Cain and Art Jackson.

Later in the Hotel Lincoln, where the Bruins stayed in those days, Frank Brimsek made the statement, "You just get established in a business like hockey and you have to give it all up. The ——— Japs bomb Pearl Harbor and a damned war comes along."

◆◆◆◆◆◆

February 11, 1942

Bruins win 8–1

Krauts on scoring spree in last game before entering military service.

The guns of war have broken up the famous Kitchener Line, formerly known as the Krauts. Last night's contest against the Canadiens at the Garden marked the Kids' final game before their entry into military service.

The game was one of the highest-scoring tilts of the season and kept the Bruins in second place.

The Bruins racked up a total of twenty-two points in goals and assists, and the Krauts were involved in half of them.

Immediately following the game's final whistle, the Montreal and Boston players lined up at center ice while the Kitchener Kids were given their military send-off.

The crowd roared its applause for the Bruins trio, who will soon see active service with the Canadian Royal Air Force. The honored Bruins, Woody Dumart, Milt Schmidt and Bobby Bauer, were presented their paychecks for the remainder of the season and a bonus.

Acting captain Jack Crawford presented his teammates with gold identification tags, known to the troops as "dog tags." Art Ross, Jr., flight officer in the Royal Air Force, and his younger brother John then presented Bauer, Dumart and Schmidt with gold chronograph wristwatches used by the Canadian Royal Air Force.

Frank Ryan, the MC, read messages from the Bruins management and Art Ross. Each word praised all three for their great team play and wished them all godspeed throughout the conflict.

At the very end of the evening, the other Bruins and Canadiens hoisted the popular players on their shoulders for the Krauts' last exit. It was a dramatic climax that left a few wet eyes in the sellout crowd.

The Kids are gone, but they shall return.

Opposite: Terry Reardon, Bill Cowley and Herb Cain, one of the Bruins lines of the early forties.

Boston's once-in-a-lifetime Krauts, on the ice.

Preceding page: *Boston Bruins, 1940–41 Stanley Cup champions.* Front row: *Frank Brimsek, Bill Cowley, Art Jackson, John Crawford, Dit Clapper, Milt Schmidt, Woody Dumart, Bobby Bauer, Eddie Wiseman.* Back row: *Mel Hill, Des Smith, Roy Conacher, Flash Hollett, Jack Shewchuk, Red Hamill, Herb Cain.*

Busher Jackson, Art Ross and
Art Jackson in 1942.

Milt Schmidt in RCAF uniform as he
enters World War II service. The
war came and took the good guys
away. Milt was one of them.

April 6, 1943

Bruins startle experts

Club that didn't figure in playoffs now fighting for Cup.

When the 1942–43 season skated off, the Bruins had no more thoughts of getting into the finals than the Americans from New York, who have now dropped out of the NHL altogether. In early games the Bruins were demolished. They had lost their good players to the war, and suddenly it seemed there were five better teams in the NHL.

All told, the Hub club had only nine players coming back from the previous season: Frank Brimsek; Dit Clapper; Bill Cowley; the Jacksons, Art and Busher; Jack Shewchuk; Jack Crawford; Herb Cain and Flash Hollett. Busher Jackson and Clapper were moving ahead in age, and Cowley had reached the not-so-magic thirties.

Jack Shewchuk, 1938–39; 1942–43—1944–45.

Art Ross was so in need of talent and bodies that he searched around wildly, willing to take anyone who could stand on skates and tape a stick handle.

Ross brought Buzz Boll, a ten-year veteran, from the defunct Americans. Boll started out like gangbusters and carried the Bruins in the early stages of the year. He didn't finish the year, as his bad knees finally conked out.

Then the B's lost Terry Reardon because he couldn't play outside Canada during the war, so Ross arranged a "quickie deal" with the Canadiens, and the Bruins came up with Murph Chamberlain. He became a valuable cog in the works during the year.

The Bruins' manager stole into the cradle and snatched up Don Gallinger, Bep Guidolin and Johnny Schmidt; the former was only seventeen, the other two eighteen. These kids were being called the Sprout Line, not quite as good as the war-departed Kraut Line.

Bill Shill appeared but stayed only a few games until he went off to the military.

When the playoffs popped up, Ross popped down to Providence and promoted that club's first line of Ab Demarco, Bill Calladine and Oscar Aubuchon. These three kids were fair-to-middlin' hockey players but not quite ripe for Stanley Cup action with the big guns from Detroit.

Ross found out that Yank Boyd was still unattached, and

Bill Cowley, 1935–36—1946–47. Hockey Hall of Fame.
Hart Trophy winner, 1940–41 and 1942–43.
Art Ross Trophy in 1940–41.

he drafted him into a Bruins uniform. Boyd at that time was nearing forty and had announced his retirement before the call from Ross came.

Detroit was a strong club, and the B's finished behind them in second spot. Clapper had missed a quarter of the year. Boll and Chamberlain were shot to pieces with injuries, and John Crawford spent a good part of the season on the sick list.

April 7, 1943

Bill Cowley gets Hart Trophy

Bill Cowley, playmaking center of the Boston Bruins, was named today as winner of the Dr. David A. Hart Trophy as the National Hockey League's most valuable player in the 1942–43 season. Cowley also won the trophy two years ago.

Cowley is a fantastic playmaker; it's been said that he's made more wings than Boeing Aircraft. Not a fast skater, he can do all kinds of things with a hockey puck. He'll give a man the puck, then take it away. He will fake a pass to the left and then pass to the right. Cowley is a man who can control the puck, coming or going.

April 8, 1943

Red Wings take Cup; beat Bruins four straight

Goalie Mowers invincible in Detroit net.

The Bruins lost their first Stanley Cup finals on Boston Garden ice last night. Johnny Mowers got his second shutout, 2–0, and gave the Detroit club a four-straight grand slam.

About 13,000 witnessed the game, the last of the 1942–43 season. It was Detroit's third Stanley Cup and a pleasurable revenge for Jack Adams and his squad, who were defeated two years ago four straight by the Bruins.

It was the third final trimming suffered by a Bruins club, who lost in 1926–27 to Ottawa and again in 1929–30 to Les Canadiens.

Detroit, promised a lot of extra dough by their home folks for four straight wins, had their hands more than full with the dynamic Bean Towners, who forced the contest to Detroit but just couldn't get by Mowers in the net.

When the Bruins had their pre-war teams they could skate with ease through most of the NHL, but none could deny the fact that the 1943 B's displayed great courage in holding off such a powerful team as the Red Wings.

As in the game the night before, the Bruins with a little luck could have pulled it out. Flash Hollett hit the post, and Cowley missed an open net, two muffs that might have pushed the series into more games.

Bill "Flash" Hollett, 1935–36—1943–44.

Top, left: *Bert Gardiner, one of five goal tenders the Bruins used during the 1943–44 season. The other net minders were Reverend George Abbott, Maurice Courteau, Jimmy Franks and Benny Grant. It must have been a tough year on goalies.*

Above: *Cooney Weiland and Art Ross during the war years.*

Toronto's Dick Irvin and Conn Smythe plotting against the Bruins at Boston Garden.

Starting the ice-making procedure for a game in the early 1940s.

Two of the best, Dit Clapper and John Crawford.

November 27, 1943 . . . . . Rossmen forced to borrow goalie—Reverend Abbott.

In 1943 the war was still raging all over the world. Many of the best NHL players were in the service, hammering away at the Germans and the Japs rather than on one another on the ice.

When Brimsek left for the U.S. Coast Guard, the Bruins had desperate problems in goal. They used five goalies throughout the year.

One night they arrived in Toronto minus a net minder. In those wartime days, each team carried only one goalie. If he got hurt, he was patched up, patted on the back, and told to return to his post. If he couldn't continue, the home team had to supply the visitors with a man for the net.

So it happened in Toronto. The Bruins were short a goalie, and the Leafs had to provide a man. Well, the Leafs weren't going to give the B's anyone good, that was for sure.

They had one man who had never played an NHL game but had been used in Leaf practice sessions. His name was George Abbott, and he was an ordained minister. The Leafs claimed that he was good—but they also admitted that he was the only man they could dig up on such short notice.

Dit Clapper found out the new man was a minister and quickly dashed into the Bruins' dressing room to warn the other players about their salty language. No cussing was to be allowed in front of the new goal tender, Reverend Abbott.

When the minister finally appeared in the dressing room, the players went to his locker and patted him on the shoulder to make him feel at home.

One of the Bruins, forgetting Dit Clapper's warning, whacked Reverend Abbott on the back with the words, "Don't worry, Abbott, we'll get those bastards. Those sons-of-bitches won't beat us."

Noting that the man of the cloth was acting slightly nervous getting dressed after his lusty welcome, Dit Clapper ventured over to him and said, "Reverend, you're not nervous, are you?"

Reverend Abbott replied to Dit, "Oh, no, no, not at all."

Clapper answered, "Well, you've got your skates on wrong. You've got the left one on your right foot and the right on your left. You'd better start over."

The minister did and skated to the net, ready for his NHL baptism.

The Leafs started right away winging shots at poor Reverend George Abbott. One vicious shot went by, and goalie Abbott turned around to look into the net to see where the puck went. The next thing he got was a shot off his rear end, which was one of his better saves of the night.

The Bruins lost the game 7–3. Perhaps Reverend Abbott was too nervous and excited to pray.

Art Jackson, 1937–38; 1939–40—1944–45.

March 5, 1944

Bruins win scoring spree 10–9

Season's smallest crowd sees Rangers edged. Cowley hits in four.

The Bruins came through this battle by the skin of their teeth. The smallest crowd of the year, fewer than 6,000, watched as a total of nineteen points went up on the scoreboard. As the score tells, Bert Gardiner in the Bruins net and his rival at the other end had off nights. Someone said the final score looked like the number of planes that the Japs had shot down in the last Pacific engagement with the U. S. Navy.

Bill Cowley had a time for himself, with four goals and two assists. In the third period, three goals were scored in thirty-seven seconds, as Kilby MacDonald had a rebound go in off his skate at the Bruins crease, Pat Egan shot one home on an Art Jackson feed, and Gauthier got his third goal of the game.

Starting lineup for the Bruins had Bep Guidolin on left wing, Cowley at center, Calladine on right wing, Clapper at left defense, Egan at right defense, and Gardiner in goal.

Charlie Scherza, Don Gallinger, Bep Guidolin, a Bruins World War II line.

Frank Brimsek.

Preceding page: *1944–45 Boston Bruins.* Front row: *Harvey Bennett, Herb Cain, Johnny Crawford, Dit Clapper, Art Ross, Bill Cowley, Pat Egan, Art Jackson.*
Back row: *Ken Smith, Billy Cupolo, Bill Jennings, Paul Gladu, Jack Shewchuk, Norm Calladine, Armand Gaudreault, Frank Mario, Gino Rozzini, Win Green.*

March 16, 1944

Red Wings top Bruins 10–9

All playoff hopes gone for Rossmen.

The Boston Bruins' Stanley Cup hopes sank tonight when they lost to Detroit in one of the highest-scoring National Hockey League games of the season. A crowd of 7,932 looked on as the Bruins counted three times in the last two and a half minutes.

Herbie Cain, stellar Bruins wingman who broke the NHL's fourteen-year-old individual scoring record recently against Chicago, counted one goal and four assists to run his grand total to eighty points.

Bill Cowley and Busher Jackson of Boston each hit three goals for the hat trick, and Carl Liscombe hammered in three for Detroit. Liscombe now has seventy points for the season.

When they were defeated tonight in Detroit, the Bruins finished their season against Detroit with only one win and two ties in ten games. Boston did not win on Detroit ice this year, which could be considered a problem.

The Bruins will certainly finish fifth for the 1943–44 season. Let's hope the war doesn't last much longer.

January 21, 1945

Bruins cut Rangers to bits 14–3

Bruins miss NHL high-scoring mark by one goal.

People left the Garden tonight after seeing the Bruins tie the NHL scoring record and come within a goal of setting a new record. The Rossmen walloped the Rangers 14–3. It was a shell-shocked evening for the poor souls from New York.

The score was 5–1 in the first period. It crept to 10–1 by the second stanza, and if the Ranger goalie hadn't made some super saves, the Bruins would have scored many more than four goals in the third period.

It wasn't much of a contest. Bill Cowley had four goals, Ken Smith had three and Mario had two.

At times during the game the Bruins lined up as in practice and just peppered the poor goal tender McAuley. It was during one of these cannon barrages that Bill Cowley scored his fourth goal of the evening's outing.

Bruins lineup: Smith, left wing; Mario, center; Cupolo, right wing; Crawford, left defense; Egan, right defense; Bibeault, goalie.

The Bruins have suffered during these war years, but the Rangers tonight seemed to be the sorriest team in the NHL.

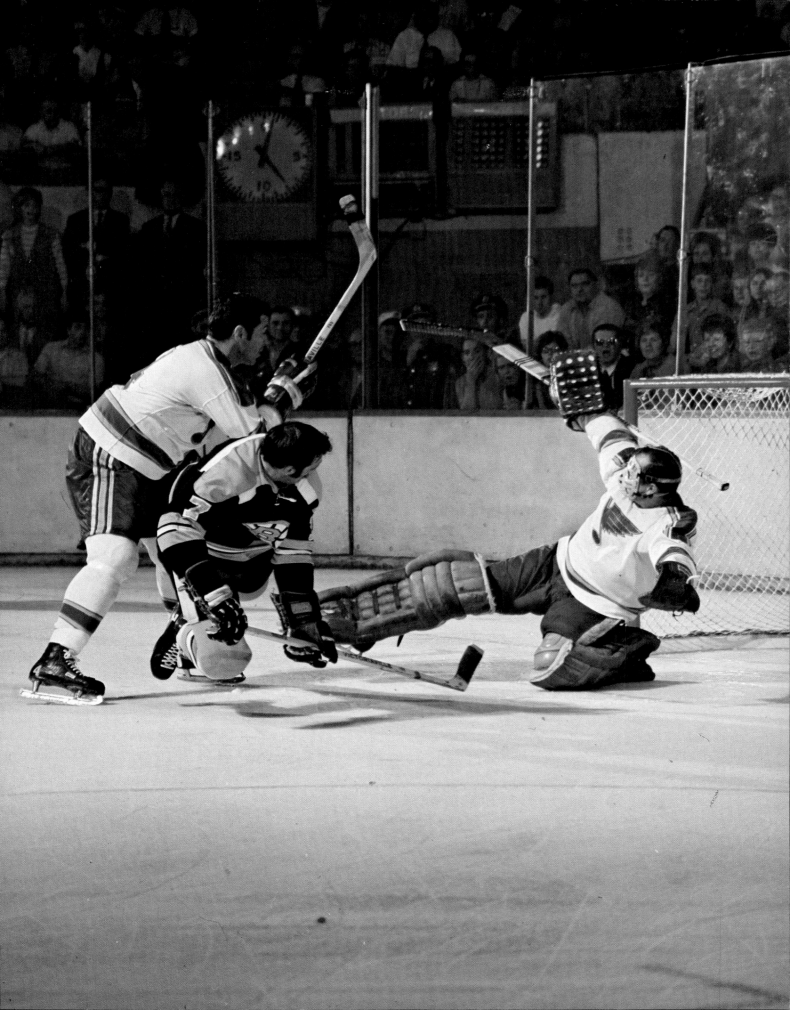

Esposito back to Bucyk in front of the St. Louis net.

St. Louis stops Fred Stanfield.

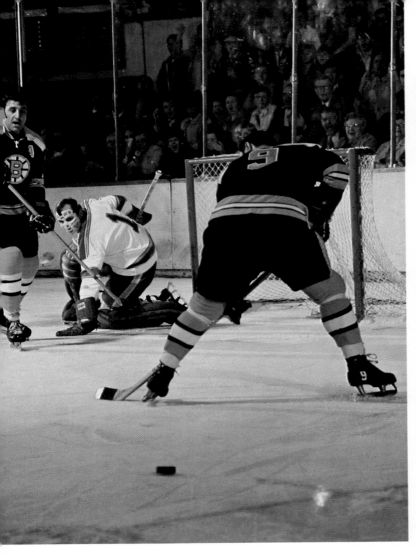

Harry Sinden studying the ice action during Stanley Cup playoffs with the Blues in 1970.

Once again, goalie Hall stops a Bruins bid.

Above: *A cause to celebrate—a Bruins playoff goal! Esposito, Sanderson and Bucyk are the happy guys.*

Opposite: *1970 playoffs. Boston's Orr, St. Louis's Hall, with Esposito of the Bruins standing by.*

Top, left: *Somewhere at the bottom is Bobby Orr, seconds after his famous 1970 playoff overtime goal.*

Middle: *Bobby Orr lands on ice after soaring through the air with his dramatic overtime goal that beat St. Louis and won the 1970 Stanley Cup.*

Right: *It's all over, and here come the fans!*

The man showing great interest in the Stanley Cup is Boston's Number 8, Ken Hodge.

Bruins fans fill Boston's streets to whoop it up for the Stanley Cup champions.

Phil Esposito holds off a Blackhawk from Chicago.

Tussle behind the net.

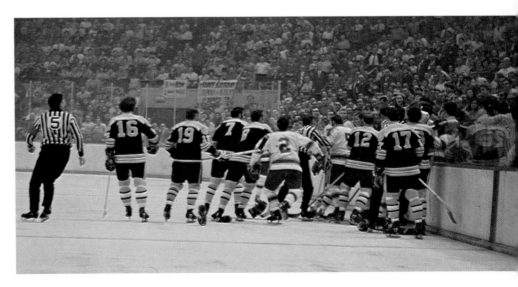

A slight discussion brewing up ice as all players prepare to man battle stations.

Opposite: *Orr and Cheevers defend the goal from Chicago attackers Hull, Mikita and White.*

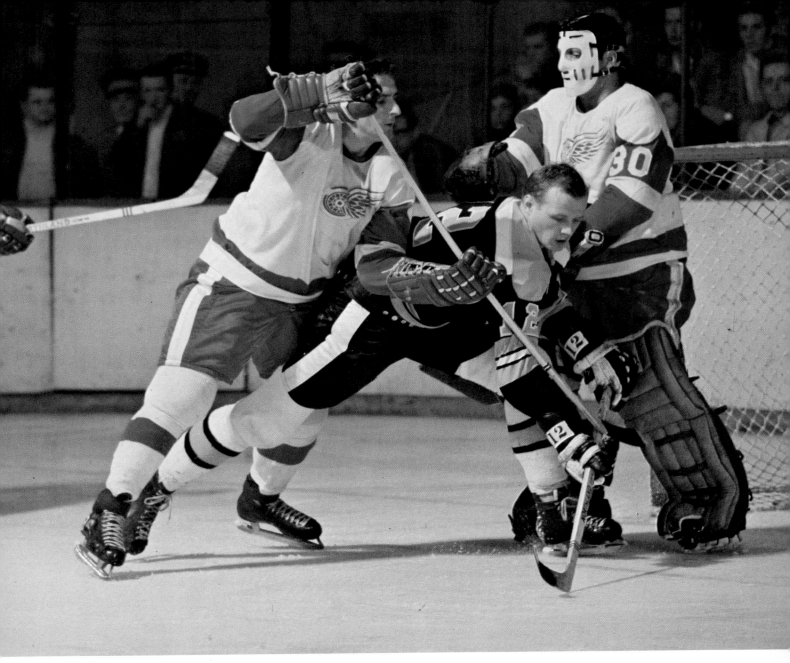

Red Wings lean on lone Bruin.

Opposite, top: *Sanderson in close and missing.*
Bottom: *Detroit's Gordie Howe and Boston's Derek Sander-son race for a loose puck.*

Above: *Bobby Orr swings into gear in the Chicago end.*

Opposite: *John McKenzie and Bobby Orr give Tony Esposito a hard time.*

Top, left: *Cheevers makes another save against the Los Angeles Kings.*

Middle: *Another game, another save.*

Right: *The Bruins and the Kings.*

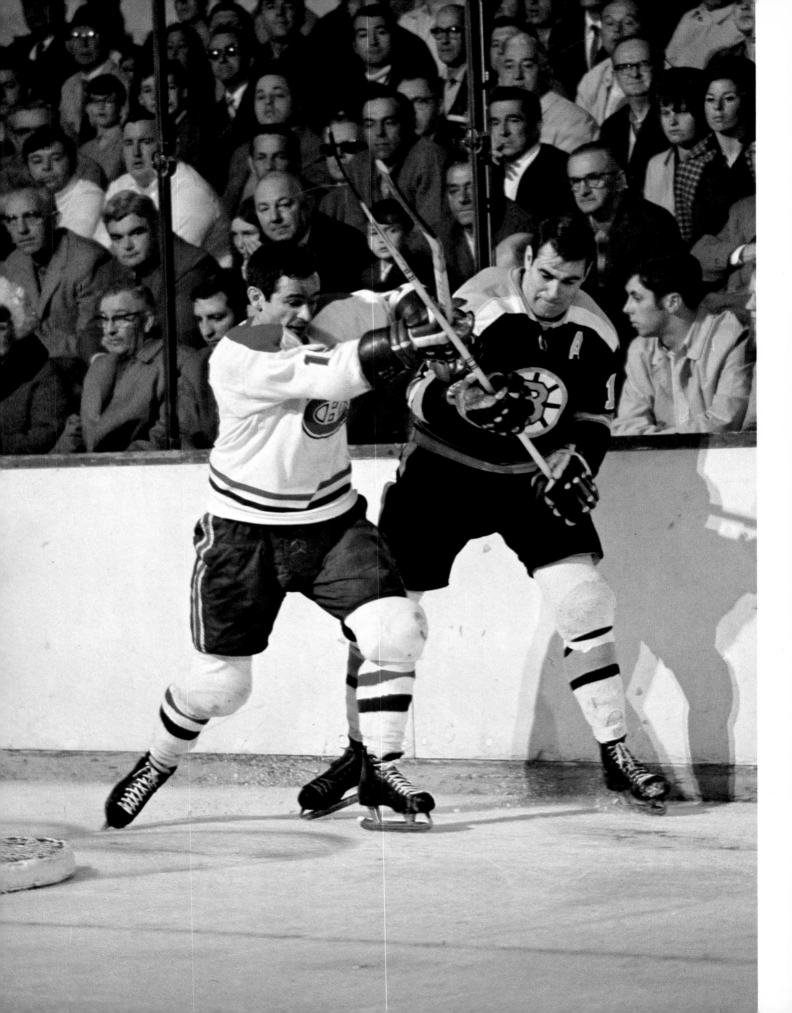

Opposite: *Jam along the boards.*

Boston-Chicago action. Bobby Orr moves quickly into position.

Roy Conacher, 1938–39—1941–42; 1945–46.

John Crawford, a sturdy rock on defense, 1938–39—1949–50.

Des Smith, 1939–40—1941–42, another member of the Bruins' defense.

Grant Warwick, 1947–48—1948–49.

Preceding page: *1948–49 Boston Bruins.*
Front row: Grant Warwick, Pete Babando,
John Crawford, Frank Brimsek, Milt Schmidt,
Pat Egan, Ken Smith.
Back row: Ed Kryzanowski, Jim Petrus, Paul
Ronty, Ed Sandford, Murray Henderson, John
Peirson, Woody Dumart, Ed Harrison,
Ferny Flaman, Dit Clapper.

Milt Schmidt signs another contract on the
dotted line, with Lynn Patrick and Art
Ross in full agreement.

Frank Brimsek.

Terry Reardon, Bill Cowley, Herb Cain.

Dit Clapper tribute tonight
Reward for twenty consecutive years with Bruins.

The Boston Bruins and the New York Rangers will face-off a National Hockey League game at Boston Garden tonight at 8:10 P.M. Before that, Dit Clapper will be honored for his twenty consecutive seasons in the NHL with the Bruins.

Ranking officials of the NHL and the International Hall of Fame and representatives of Canadian amateur hockey have come to Boston for this most unusual ceremony.

The ice ceremonies will consist of four presentations. Clapper will be officially notified of his election to the International Hockey Hall of Fame by its president, J. Stuart Crawford, Mayor of Kingston, Ontario, where the hall is located. Colonel Clarence Campbell, president of the NHL, will present Clapper with a silver service. Julius F. Haller and Edmond F. Dagnino will present the fans' gift of United States Treasury bonds, and William Grimes will present the gift of the past and present Boston hockey writers. Dit Clapper will skate out on the ice tonight wearing his old jersey number 5, and his knees will be shaking like they did that cold day in 1927 when he reported to the Bruins wearing a fancy checked cap, high boots and a jazzbo tie.

The Bruins are tied for third place with forty-one points, three and a half games ahead of Detroit. The Bruins have fifteen games to play, and the Rangers, who are also tied for third, have sixteen to go.

The Bruins will start the Kraut Line against New York, with Jack Crawford and Ferny Flaman on defense and Brimsek in goal.

Dit Clapper.

Opposite: Garden game in the 1950s.

The
Quiet Fifties

Bill Ezinicki, Milt Schmidt and Woody Dumart in 1952.

March 17, 1952

Bruins beat Hawks 4–0
Playoff spot assured.

Captain Milt Schmidt scored his two hundredth major league goal and his Kraut linemates Bobby Bauer and Woody Dumart played stellar games as the Bruins won entrance to the playoffs for the twenty-third year in twenty-eight tries by blanking Chicago 4–0 before 12,658 fans at the Garden, the second largest turnout of the season.

Schmidt's goal brought the crowd to their feet at 12:58 in the second period. A second rousing ovation greeted Bobby Bauer's goal at 6:40 in the final period. This was Bauer's first Bruin game after a five-year absence. He had been keeping in shape playing amateur hockey in Kitchener, Ontario, and returned to the Bruins for this one game. Bauer jumped into the Hawks net to scoop up the

Milt Schmidt and Woody Dumart.

puck as a souvenir for Milt after Schmidt had scored his big two hundredth marker.

Bauer started the game with his former teammates Schmidt and Dumart, but Kryzanowski frequently took over before their turn was up, as Bobby was inclined to tire. Bauer showed plenty of finesse, however, and brought the following postgame comment from Lynn Patrick: "I wish I'd had him for the last five years."

When the game ended, Bauer skated back down the ice to congratulate Jim Henry, who came through with his seventh Bruins shutout. Henry skated to center ice to extend his congratulations to Schmidt.

Schmidt's first goal for the Bruins was on March 12, 1937, against the same Hawks in Chicago, where Boston won 6–2. Milt had stick-handled through Art Wiebe and Earl Siebert, a pair of rugged defense men, for a solo goal. The Chicago press had reported, "Wiebe and Siebert went out for a cup of coffee while a youngster named Schmidt scored for

Boston." Now, fifteen years later, he notched his two hundredth.

A club movement was started to have Bauer finish out the season with the Bruins, but Bauer felt that he could not afford to stay away from his skate business. "It was a wonderful experience," puffed Bobby Bauer when the game was over. "I'll never forget it." And neither will the Boston fans who were there on that memorable night.

Referee Gravel and linesmen Babcock and Morrison wore the new bright orange NHL officials' sweaters. As they skated onto the ice they were roasted with derisive hoots from the ticket holders. Organist John Kiley added a humorous touch by playing "The Wearing of the Green."

March 17, 1952: The Bruins' Kraut Line play last game together as a unit. Bobby Bauer came out of retirement to skate one more time with his mates, Milt Schmidt and Woody Dumart.

April 6, 1953

Bruins win entry to Stanley Cup finals

Whack out early lead over Wings and hang in for 4–2 victory.

The Boston Bruins authored one of the biggest surprises in NHL history as they headed for the Stanley Cup championship round for the first time since 1943 by decking the once-invincible Detroit Red Wings 4–2 before a wild, shouting crowd of 13,909 last night at the Garden.

The Bruins did something the experts said would never happen: they beat the Detroit supermen. Next come the finals against the winner of the Montreal-Chicago series.

The Red Wings were last year's Stanley Cup champs. They had run all over regular league competition to carry the NHL pace for the past five weeks. Detroit was being hailed as the greatest hockey team in the history of the game, but last night the Bruins spoiled all those thoughts.

The tension-packed third period is one that Bruins fans will be talking about for the next one hundred years. The Bruins beat back countless attacks by the fighting Red Wings from Detroit. Jim Henry, reliable Bruins goalie, made forty-two saves during the night's contest. He stopped seventeen in the third period, when the Red Wings seemed sure to tie up the game.

Jim Henry, Bruins goal tender, shakes hands with Maurice "Rocket" Richard after dramatic 1953 Stanley Cup finals against Montreal. Bruins lost final game 1–0 after lone goal by the famous Rocket. Henry is spotting a couple of shiners, and Richard doesn't look too hot, either.

1953 playoffs . . . . . Hockey's first shadows show up.

Lynn Patrick was a coach who would fit a player to a certain purpose. It didn't matter if the player was a veteran or a rookie; if a need arose, that man played.

Before the opening game of the series, the Bruins held a meeting, and Patrick told his team, "Don't worry, we're going to show them a thing or two. We'll have a few tricks up our sleeves." Patrick's game plan was to stop Gordie Howe and Ted Lindsay. He figured that if the Bruins could handle these two they could handle the entire Detroit team.

And what developed was hockey's first "shadow." Patrick assigned Woody Dumart, who was a good defensive player, to do nothing but check Gordie Howe. And Joe Klukay was to do nothing but check Lindsay, with Milt Schmidt the swing man. That was all they were supposed to do. But somehow Howe and Lindsay ducked their "shadows," and Detroit won the first game, with the Bruins on the short end 7–0.

The Bruins were downcast when Patrick called another meeting. "Don't worry, we'll be all right. We just have to make a few adjustments—we'll be ready for the next game."

The Bruins adjusted to the new game plan. Woody stuck to Howe like glue, never letting him touch the puck. Patrick had told him, "If Howe goes to the men's room, you go with him."

After the series was over, Howe announced that he was going to get married. Woody came out with a great crack: "Here I've been so close to Howe all during the past two weeks, and he didn't even tell me about it."

The close-checking Bruins upset Detroit in six games.

April 16, 1953 . . . . . Bruins lose to Canadiens.

On the day of the final Stanley Cup game in Montreal, Jim Henry, the Bruins' goal tender, came up with two badly swollen eyes. They were so black and puffy that he had to keep cold compresses on them the entire day.

Lynn Patrick had to make the decision of either going with a different goalie who could see or using Henry, with his bad eyes.

Henry played, bad eyes and all. He saw all the pucks except one. And that was all Montreal needed to win, 1–0.

Preceding page: *Teams stand at attention on Boston Garden ice for the playing of the National Anthem.*

Joe Klukay, 1952–53—1954–55.

1953 photo of Hay Laycoe, Lynn Patrick
and Milt Schmidt.

John Peirson, Ed Sandford, Dave
Creighton, 1953 Bruins.

Milt Schmidt, Walter Brown and Lynn Patrick hold a press conference in the late fifties.

◆◆◆◆◆◆◆

December 1954 . . . . . Milt Schmidt retires.

Milt retired in December 1954, just around Christmas. He had suffered so many injuries during his long career that he decided it was time to hang up his skates.

Lynn Patrick moved on to general manager of the Bruins, and Milt became the new bench boss. When Milt took over as coach, Patrick authored the famous quote, "Milt Schmidt will never be as good a coach as I was." Asked why, Patrick replied, "Because he'll never be able to look down the bench when in trouble and yell, 'Schmidt, get out there and take care of things!' "

Patrick could always count on Milt Schmidt, the player. Now Coach Milt Schmidt wouldn't have a Milt Schmidt to take him out of trouble.

◆◆◆◆◆◆◆

Milt Schmidt holds up his super number 15 to Larry Regan, Bruins' Calder Trophy winner, 1956–57.

John Peirson, Fleming Mackell, Jim Henry and Leo LaBine in Bruins dressing room in the mid-fifties.

◆◆◆◆◆◆◆

1956–57 season . . . . . Terry Sawchuk takes off.

Before the beginning of the 1955–56 season, the Detroit Red Wings traded Terry Sawchuk to the Boston Bruins for five players. When Detroit let Sawchuk go, they said his nerves had gotten the better of him.

Sawchuk had played for the Bruins for about a year when he walked out at mid-season, saying he was sick with mononucleosis. Actually, Sawchuk had some personal problems.

When it all happened, General Manager Lynn Patrick was out in Winnipeg on a scouting trip. Coach Milt Schmidt was laid up at home with the flu. Herb Ralby of the Boston Globe, who worked part-time with the Bruins as PR man, remembers, "I was told to get down to the Garden and find Sawchuk, that he had just walked out on the club. I found Sawchuk but couldn't talk him out of leaving."

Sawchuk had walked in on Walter Brown and said, "I'm sick. I want to quit, and that's it."

Walter Brown told him, "Well, I would never keep anybody who doesn't want to stay. I'll go and get the money that's due you."

Sawchuk stayed out the rest of the season, and later threatened to sue some of the Boston writers who had said he really didn't have mononucleosis.

◆◆◆◆◆◆◆

Following page: Late 1950s Bruins game at Boston Garden.

Ferny Flaman, Jean Beliveau from Montreal and Terry Sawchuk share a few thoughts in 1956. Sawchuk, on the right, departed from the Bruins on his own during the 1956–57 season.

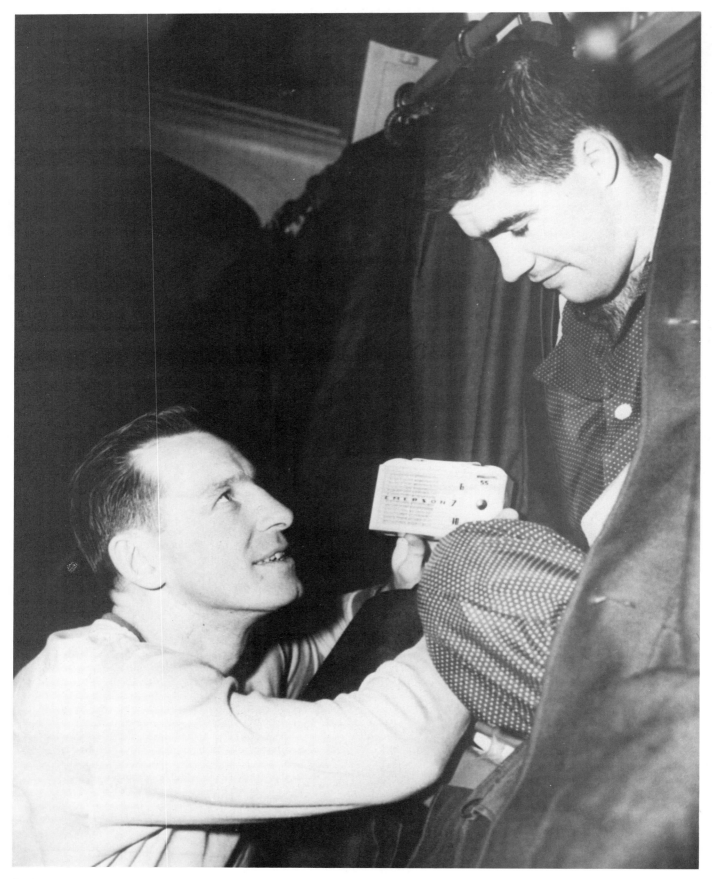

*Riding the rails with the Bruins in the fifties as Fleming
Mackell, in his pajamas, gets the good word from
Milt Schmidt.*

Jerry Toppazzini, Ed Sandford and Dave Creighton, Bruins players in the fifties. Toppazzini would extend his career into the early sixties.

Leo LaBine.

Not only was Leo LaBine a good hard-hitting hockey player; he was a good man to have around to lighten the spirits of the team.

One day in Boston, during the mid-1950s, after Milt Schmidt became coach, the Bruins were sitting in their dressing room after a practice session.

Milt, who used to wear a soft wide-brimmed hat, ventured into the room to give the boys a talk.

"Let's concentrate on hockey for a change and stop the fooling around." After a few other words of encouragement, Schmidt turned to leave the room.

That's all Leo LaBine needed. He had been curling up a large roll of used tape into a ball, and he let it go at the back of Milt's head.

The man in the soft hat turned quickly, with fire in his eyes. "Who did that?"

LaBine yelled, "Hey, Topper [Jerry Toppazzini], what did you do that for?"

Everyone knew who did it, and even Milt Schmidt started to laugh.

Another time, after his retirement, Leo was asked during a TV interview in Toronto, "Leo, do you think the game is as rough as in the old days?" Leo didn't want to answer any questions about rough stuff in hockey, but the announcer insisted. "Leo, do you think hockey roughness is any different now from what it was before?" Still Leo ignored the question. Finally the guy asked, "Leo, if you were playing today, what would you do differently?"

LaBine thought for a moment. "Well, I'd go to more parties and stay a little longer."

Following page: *The 1958–59 Bruins.*
Front row: *Don Simmons, Fleming Mackell, President Walter A. Brown, Coach Milt Schmidt, General Manager Lynn Patrick, Captain Ferny Flaman, Harry Lumley*
Middle row: *Doug Mohns, Don McKenney, Vic Stasiuk, Larry Leach, Bob Armstrong, Jerry Toppazzini, Gordon Redahl, Leo LaBine*
Back row: *Trainer Hammy Moore, Leo Boivin, Earl Reibel, John Bucyk, Larry Hillman, Bronco Horvath, Jim Morrison, Guy Gendron*

Willie O'Ree, first black player in the NHL and Bruins member, 1957–58—1960–61.

John ''Chief'' Bucyk skated into the Bruins picture from Detroit in 1957–58.

Ferny Flaman, 1945–46—1950–51; 1954–55—1960–61.

Vic Stasiuk, member of the Bruins' Uke Line, in his off-season uniform.

Vic Stasiuk, member of the Bruins' Uke Line, in his working uniform.

Bruins' Uke Line—Vic Stasiuk, Bronco Horvath
and John Bucyk—in 1959.

The Uke Line.

The nickname "Uke Line" was created by Herb Ralby,
who hung the tag on Vic Stasiuk, John Bucyk and
Bronco Horvath. They played together as a line in the
mid-fifties. Stasiuk and Bucyk were Ukrainians, and
Horvath said he didn't mind being called one to complete
the nickname.

The boys all lived together during those early years,
and Horvath, being the cook, always managed to come
up with lima beans before every game. Perhaps another
good nickname for them would have been the Lima Line.

◆◆◆◆◆◆

Good Times in the Sixties

Bruins' dressing room in 1965. Old-timer Dit Clapper checks a skate edge, with trainers Hammy Moore, left, and Win Green offering some advice.

Bronco Horvath.

There was a time in 1960, during the last game of the season, when Bronco Horvath was leading the NHL scoring parade by one point over Bobby Hull. The Bruins were playing Chicago in their final game of the season at the Garden.

In the first period, Bob Armstrong let go a shot from the blue line that hit Bronco in the jaw and knocked him out. They decided to rush Horvath to the hospital to see if his jaw was shattered.

Horvath kept exclaiming, "I want to play, I want to play," and he didn't even take off his uniform on the fast trip to the hospital.

At the hospital they took some X-rays and found that the jaw was bruised but not broken.

Horvath was rushed back to the Garden, where he played the third period. But while he was off visiting the medics, Hull had come up with two points and had beaten Bronco for the NHL title.

One that got away: Bernie Parent, with Milt Schmidt, in 1965.

Don McKenney, Bruins player, 1954–55—1962–63. Winner of the Lady Byng Trophy for most gentlemanly player, 1959–60.

1955 charity golf match, with participants Milt Schmidt and John Peirson.

Following page: *1962–63 Bruins.*
Front row: *Bob Perreault, Forbes Kennedy, Captain Leo Boivin, Don McKenney, Wayne Hicks, Bob Leiter, Ed Johnston*
Middle row: *Guy Gendron, Ted Green, Irwin Spencer, Coach Milt Schmidt, Charlie Burns, Murray Oliver, Trainer Win Green*
Back row: *John Bucyk, Doug Mohns, Warren Godfrey, Ed Westfall, Tom Williams, Jerry Toppazzini*

August 5, 1964

Bruins' Art Ross dies

Art Ross, former Bruins coach and general manager, died this morning at the Emery Nursing Home in West Medford, Massachusetts, after a long illness.

Ross's hockey career spanned fifty-nine years. He joined the Boston team in 1924 and remained with the organization until 1954.

As a young man, he learned to skate with blades made by the Ojibway Indians, and his first hockey teammates were the same braves.

He became one of Canada's top athletes in hockey and baseball. In 1907 Ross was paid one thousand dollars a game for two games by the Kenora Thistles for a championship series. That was big pay when you consider Ross's yearly salary as a bank clerk was only six hundred dollars.

Mr. Hockey died today.

Art Ross, top row, left, member of the 1908–09 Cobalt Hockey Club in Canada.

Leighton "Hap" Emms, Bruins player, 1934–35, and later general manager. Emms was the man who signed Bobby Orr to his first Bruins contract, in 1966.

June 13, 1966

Bruins GM confident about signing Orr

Bruins General Manager Hap Emms revealed today that he doesn't anticipate any trouble in signing Bobby Orr, the eighteen-year-old amateur whiz, and that the young lad would, if he signs, be at the Bruins' London, Ontario, training camp this fall. "I talked with Bobby two or three weeks ago," Emms said. "He has not demanded anything. We'll do more than our share to make him happy."

Emms told Bobby to call him anytime he was ready to talk contract. Hap figures it probably won't be until sometime in August that they will get together. Orr is still eligible for three more years of Junior Amateur Hockey with the Oshawa Generals.

The Bruins, however, won't register the official pact with the NHL office until Bobby proves he's ready for major league competition. That way he will still be eligible to return to Oshawa.

Bobby Orr.

◆◆◆◆◆◆

Bobby Orr.

The Bruins first came into contact with Bobby Orr around 1961 during a Canadian scouting expedition by Lynn Patrick, Wren Blair, Weston Adams, Harold Cotton and Bucky Kane. They found Bobby quite by accident. They had had some reports on a youngster named Eaton, whose team was playing a youth hockey game against a team from Parry Sound, Ontario. Once they spotted Bobby playing on the Parry Sound club, they stopped looking at Eaton and focused all attention on young Robert Gordon Orr.

They all agreed: "We have got to get this kid, no matter what."

Wren Blair was assigned the task of coordinating hockey functions with Bobby's parents, Doug and Arva Orr.

Lynn Patrick said at the time, "I may not be here, but once Bobby Orr comes to Boston, you'll have nothing but winning teams."

The Boston Bruins signed Orr to a contract in June 1966 on Emms's boat in Canada.

◆◆◆◆◆◆

Bobby Orr getting his playing gear ready in the dressing room during his rookie season (1966–67).

Bobby Orr as a junior, in his Oshawa Generals uniform.

June 1966

Bobby Orr likened to Gordie Howe

Wren Blair of the Bruins organization recently said, "You won't find many kids like Bobby Orr. I just hope the Boston fans realize when they see him that he's just a human being. They shouldn't expect him to dominate the pros at the start, as he did with the juniors. That's just asking too much."

Because of Orr's great offensive talent, some people have said he should be playing forward. In fact, during Orr's bantam and midget years, his father, Doug, asked Orr's coach, Bucko MacDonald, to move Bobby up front.

The old pro told Doug Orr, "Anybody can be a forward, but there aren't too many superstar defense men."

Lynn Patrick, formerly with the Bruins, paid Bobby Orr a real compliment by comparing him with the now-famous Gordie Howe of Detroit.

Orr scored thirty, thirty-four and thirty-eight goals his last three years of playing defense in the OHA.

He's anxiously awaiting the Bruins' training camp in London, Ontario, this fall. "I want to find out how I stack up with the pros," said Bobby Orr.

Bobby Orr signs his first Bruins contract in June 1966, with advice from his attorney, Alan Eagleson. The big event took place in Canada on General Manager Hap Emms's boat.

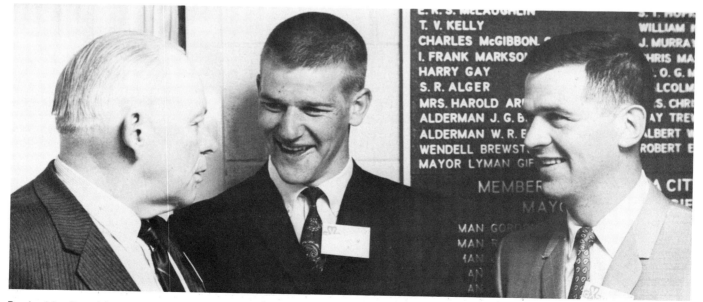

Bucko MacDonald, one of Bobby Orr's first coaches; Orr; and Harry Sinden, in 1966.

Opposite: Orr battles Montreal's Beliveau for the puck during a January 1967 game.

Harry Sinden behind the bench
in a 1966–67 game.

June 14, 1966

NHL expansion clubs also sought Bruins' new coach, Sinden

Harry Sinden could have had the coaching job with either of two expansion teams if the Bruins hadn't grabbed him first. The Bruins' new bench boss is held in high regard by Wren Blair, former Bruins farm system executive.

Blair, a close friend of Sinden and a man who brought him into the Boston organization six years ago, described the thirty-three-year-old Boston pilot as a strong-willed individual who can handle players. "He'll be firm with his men," Blair said, "but he'll have the players' respect."

Sinden, who succeeds Milt Schmidt as the Bruins coach, played seven years for Blair, and, as Blair stated, "He was always my star defense man and captain. He was the leader."

Their close association started when Blair positioned Sinden on the Whitby Ontario Dunlops, who won the world title in 1958, beating Russia and Czechoslovakia.

Later Blair managed the Kingston Frontenacs for the Bruins. Here Sinden turned pro in 1960–61 and was immediately made captain. Two years later Harry Sinden was appointed player-coach, a job he continued in Minneapolis and last season for the champion Oklahoma City Blazers.

Sinden comes to the Bruins with vast hockey knowledge.

May 16, 1967

Bruins swap three for three with Chicago

The Bruins, needing some strength down the center slot and some size up front, today announced a major trade with the Chicago Blackhawks.

Centers Phil Esposito and Fred Stanfield will come to Boston with big right winger Ken Hodge. Going in the other direction will be Giles Marotte, Pit Martin and minor league goalie Jack Norris.

The deal was completed just before all rosters were frozen for the expansion draft.

Milt Schmidt, Bruins general manager, had been planning this arrangement for some time. When Chicago Coach Tommy Ivan's phone call came through from Florida with the final okay, Milt's face lit up like a Christmas tree.

The general manager said, "We gained needed strength up front as well as size. We hated to give up Marotte, but we had to give up something to get what we wanted."

The 6-foot, 187-pound Esposito is twenty-five and for the past three years has been centering for Bobby Hull and Chico Maki. During those three years he notched seventy-one goals.

Hodge, twenty-two, is a big, tough customer who can score goals. He'll get more ice time with the Bruins, where he won't have to play behind Chico Maki and Kenny Wharram.

Schmidt feels that Stanfield could be a real sleeper in the deal.

May 16, 1967

Coach Sinden's view on trade

Harry Sinden of the Bruins was at a banquet at the Royal Military College in Kingston, Ontario, when he learned of the big three-for-three trade the Bruins made with Chicago.

His reaction was the same as if he had been in Boston: "It should help us to get into the playoffs—we got something to build three lines around."

The Bruins succeeded in trading for physical strength down the middle without giving away anything in their youth program. The trade is actually a two-for-three deal, because Norris has had only a brief run in the NHL.

Sinden was well aware the trade was in the making and was consulted by General Manager Milt Schmidt and his predecessor, Hap Emms.

This is how Sinden looked at the departure of Marotte: "Chicago is not the team for us to worry about. They're out there by twenty points, and the addition of Marotte, even if he puts them out there by thirty points, doesn't mean as much as it would have had we given him to New York or Detroit or Toronto."

Phil Esposito, who became the Bruins' big scorer after the big trade with Chicago in May 1967.

Ken Hodge, who also came to the B's from the Hawks in 1967.

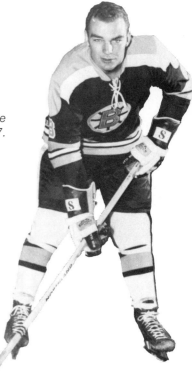

Below: *Phil Esposito, Derek Sanderson, Eddie Shack and Fred Stanfield getting the feel of Boston Garden ice in 1967.*

Espo and Derek Sanderson sitting on the net instead of shooting at it.

Following page: 1967 Bruins-Leafs game. Bobby gets some aid from Gary Doak.

Bruins lose season's finale to Leafs 4–1
Esposito scores.

The Bruins were on the short end in their final game of the regular season, but it didn't upset the 14,310 onlookers.

The Bruins had clinched third place and were getting set for the opening gun of the Stanley Cup with Montreal.

The big center of the Bruins, Phil Esposito, received both the Dufresne and the Eddie Shore trophies. And tension was riding high among the fans to see if Number 7 or Chicago's Stan Mikita would win the Art Ross individual-scoring trophy.

The 14,310 set off a mighty howl when Esposito scored the only Bruin tally at 9:53 in the third period.

That tied Phil and Mikita at eighty-four points each. Harry Sinden helped Phil out with extra line changes and gave him a solid tour of four minutes' duty at the finish.

Shortly after the Bruins left the ice, it was announced by Frank Fallon that Mikita got an assist against Detroit in Chicago to make him the official winner with eighty-five points.

The Bruins put forth some extra efforts, most notably Bobby Orr, wheeling and dealing in his dazzling style. Teddy Green also played a good game.

When Esposito took the Dufresne Trophy for best performance on home ice, he said, "I hope this won't give anybody the impression I'm just a homer."

The game was the thirty-second sellout in thirty-seven games, bringing the Bruins' attendance to a new high of 500,000 for the regular season.

*Sanderson, Shack, Sinden, Stanfield, Esposito—
1967 practice session.*

Orr on ice in a game with Detroit. Gordie Howe stands ready, and again Doak helps out, with Ed Johnston guarding the B's net.

March 3, 1969

Espo scores 2

Bruins romp 4–0.

Phil Esposito, the big man with the curved hockey blade, became the first player in NHL history to score 100-plus points when he notched his thirty-ninth and fortieth goals of the season to lead the Bruins to a 4–0 victory over Pittsburgh.

Another sellout throng of 14,659 gave Espo a five-minute standing ovation, strewing the ice with hats and assorted bric-a-brac after his record-making goals.

"We want Espo! We want Espo!" the fans chanted in unison. Phil finally took a brief spin to mid-ice to keep his 14,659 admirers happy.

Espo's goals were beauties, especially the second, which occurred while the Bruins were killing off a penalty to Rick Smith.

After just seventeen seconds of the third period, Ted Green, another of the game's stars, fed a pass to Hodge. Hodge relayed to Espo, steaming in on goalie Joe Daley, and he slid the puck right under the Pittsburgh net minder.

Hats, programs, ice cream boxes, a white football hat and even one brassiere came showering down on the ice. Espo, a broad grin across his face, came to the Boston bench and flipped the souvenir puck to the assistant trainer, John Forristall.

Meanwhile, teammates thumped the 6-foot, 1-inch, 205-pound center on the back and happily shook his hand.

Following page: Espo lets one go at Ed Giacomin of the Rangers.

131

Bobby Orr and Derek Sanderson.

April 29, 1969

Esposito and Orr get awards

The National Hockey League awarded its top trophies to two Bruins players for outstanding service during the regular season.

The Hart Trophy, given to the most valuable player to his team for the 1968–69 season, went to Esposito, the Boston Bruins center who won the league's scoring championship with 126 points during the year.

The James Norris Trophy was picked up by Bobby Orr, all-star Bruins player, as best defense man of the year. Orr had the largest margin of victory, with 176 points. Next defense man in line was Tim Horton of Toronto, with 48 points. The winners were chosen by a vote of the National Hockey League Writers Association.

It was the first time since 1952–53 that the winners were selected in only one poll at the end of the season. In the previous fifteen years, the selections were made in two polls, one at mid-season and the other at the end of the regular season.

Bobby Orr with just two of his many trophies.

Boston's famous Number 4.

Ted Green.

September 1969 . . . . . Wayne Maki-Ted Green incident, Ottawa.

During a pre-season game with the St. Louis Blues in Ottawa, Ted Green, the Bruins' tough defense man, took Wayne Maki hard into the corner boards. Maki, bouncing back off the boards, made a spearing motion at Green with his stick. Ted brought up his stick; Maki raised his, and as he did, it glanced off Green's stick and hit the Bruins player on the head.

Green suffered serious injuries, and his life hung in the balance for many days.

He recovered and after a very long absence rejoined the Bruins and later transferred to the WHA.

Wayne Maki slashes at Ted Green with his stick. Green is on the right with his hands up.

Phil Esposito.

136

The Powerhouse Seventies

Bruins' Stanley Cup runneth Orr

Bobby Orr scored a goal forty seconds into sudden-death overtime today that brought the Stanley Cup to Boston for the first time in twenty-nine years.

Orr's super goal made the Bruins champions of the world.

Orr, more than any other individual on the team, contributed to the Bruins' success in the series.

In the overtime, Orr made a daring dash from the blue line deep into St. Louis territory to beat Larry Keenan to the loose puck. Bobby knocked the puck behind the net to Derek Sanderson and broke for the Blues' net.

Sanderson gave Orr a perfect pass, and as goal tender Glenn Hall moved across the net, Orr jammed the puck between the veteran's legs.

After scoring the goal, Orr bounded through the air in a superman leap. "It's so great! It's so great!" he kept repeating, shaking his head in disbelief of what he had done.

"I saw it go in. Oh yeah, it was in. I didn't know where it was going. I just shot the darn thing. I think it went between his [Hall's] legs. I have to be the luckiest guy in the world."

It was that kind of a Stanley Cup finish for the Bruins. Several records were broken and others equaled.

Minutes after Orr's goal, John Bucyk was skating around Boston Garden ice with Lord Stanley's cup in his arms.

The crowd roared its full approval of the entire proceedings.

Weston Adams said, "We have a great hockey team. There is no thrill in sports like winning the Stanley Cup. We have a team we can be proud of. I'm very happy."

The Bruins' dressing room was bedlam. Wayne Cashman kept sipping champagne from the treasured Stanley Cup.

Coach Harry Sinden was soaking wet after the players tossed him and Weston Adams, Jr., into the shower.

Johnny "Pie" McKenzie was squirting everybody in sight with a magnum of champagne.

All over the Bruins' dressing room the celebration continued. Players tripped over television cables and reporters in their happy search for more bubble bottles.

Orr was displaying a shirt he had on under his jersey. It read: BOSTON BRUINS . . . 1970 STANLEY CUP CHAMPIONS.

Boston Garden ice, meanwhile, was littered with hats, streamers, papers, beer cans and a thousand other items.

It was Boston's happiest day.

Preceding page: It's May 10, 1970, and Bobby "Superman" Orr leaps through space after scoring famous overtime goal to clinch the Stanley Cup against the St. Louis Blues in Boston.

Milt Schmidt, Tom Johnson, Bobby Orr and Harry Sinden huddle around the Cup with victory smiles in 1970.

Liquid goodies in the Stanley Cup get dumped on Bobby Orr's head.

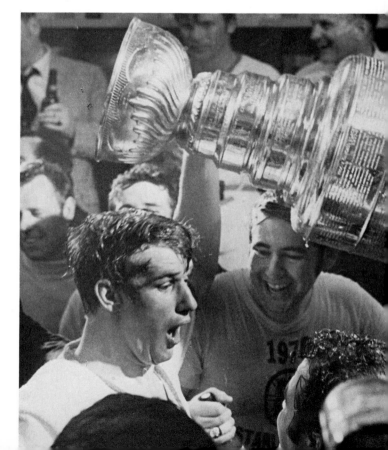

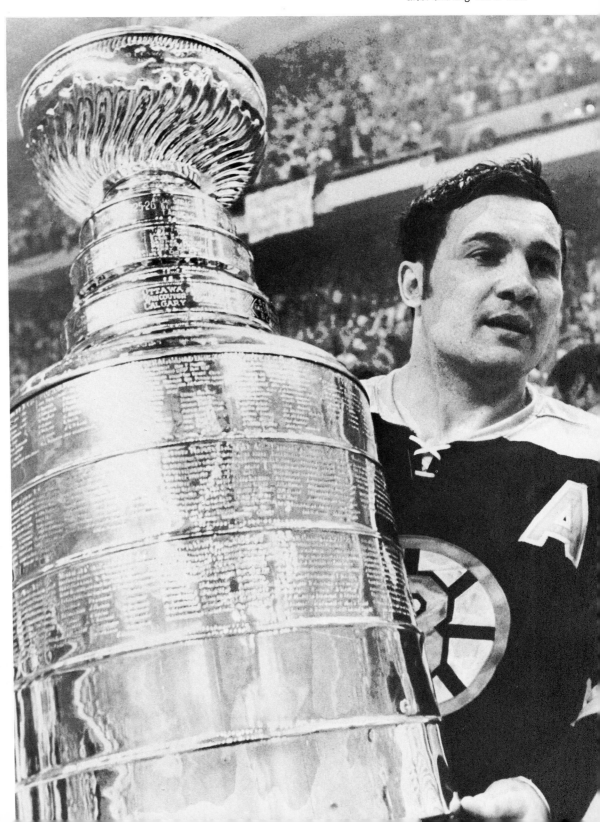

John Bucyk skates the Stanley Cup around Boston Garden
after the big 1970 win.

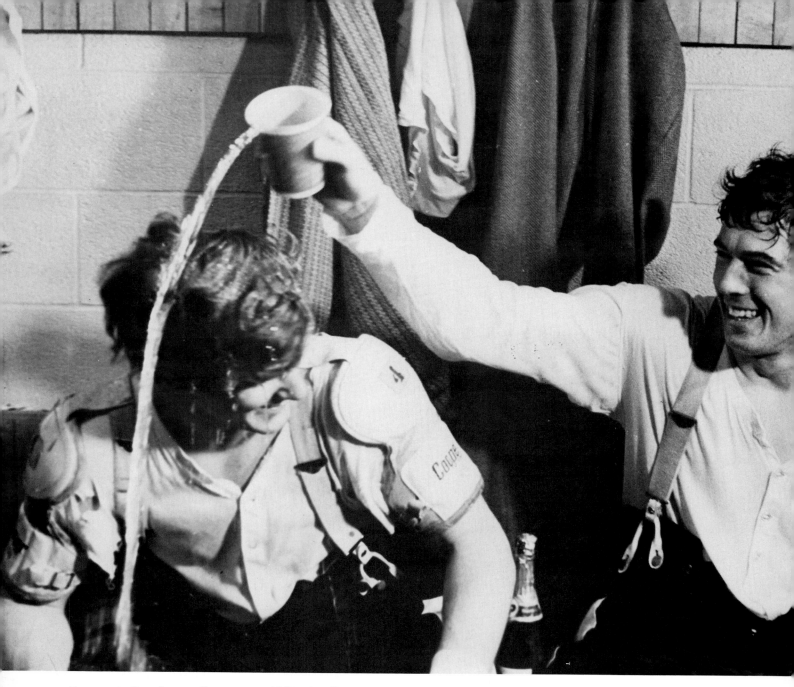

Teammate Don Awrey slips some cold Stanley Cup
beverage over Orr.

Following page: *1969–70 Boston Bruins, Stanley Cup champions.*
Front row: Gerry Cheevers, General Manager Milt Schmidt, Coach Harry Sinden, Ed Johnston, Chairman of the Board Weston W. Adams, President Weston W. Adams, Jr., Assistant to General Manager Tom Johnson, John Adams
Middle row: Trainer Dan Canney, Bill Lesuk, Bobby Orr, Wayne Cashman, Ed Westfall, Phil Esposito, Don Awrey, Don Marcotte, John Bucyk, Fred Stanfield, Assistant Trainer John Forristall
Back row: John McKenzie, Ron Murphy, Dallas Smith, Derek Sanderson, Wayne Carleton, Ken Hodge, Bill Speer, Garnet Bailey, Gary Doak, Jim Lorentz, Rick Smith

John "Pie" McKenzie enjoys a few sips of champagne.

Milt Schmidt congratulates Tom Johnson, new Bruins coach for 1970–71 season.

May 14, 1970

Harry Sinden quits as Bruins coach

Coach Harry Sinden today retired from the Boston Bruins and professional hockey. His retirement comes just four days after Boston's first Stanley Cup in twenty-nine years.

Harry says he plans to enter private business. It is believed he will take a position in the home-development field.

June 1970

Tom Johnson named B's coach

The new coach of the Boston Bruins, Tom Johnson, is a member of Hockey's Hall of Fame and has played on six Stanley Cup teams while with the Montreal Canadiens. He spent fifteen years in the NHL, the final two with the Bruins.

Harry Sinden.

Bruins knocked out of playoffs by Habs
Goalie Dryden shuts door again.

Ken Dryden, the 6-foot, 4-inch rookie goal tender with the lightning-fast hand, led the Montreal Canadiens to a 4–2 victory over the Bruins yesterday afternoon at the Boston Garden. Montreal won the Stanley Cup quarterfinals in the seventh game.

Coach Tom Johnson said, "The Canadiens got terrific goal tending, and they skated like hell. They forechecked us to death in the third period."

"How can a guy like that [Dryden] play like that for so many games?" asked General Manager Milt Schmidt.

Aggressive John McKenzie, tugging off a sweaty undershirt, said Dryden "was simply fantastic."

"He's got a *bleeping* good hand," said the Young Turk, Derek Sanderson.

The Bruins, defending Stanley Cup champions, zoomed forty-eight shots at Dryden, a twenty-three-year-old McGill University law student, and managed to beat him only on goals by John Bucyk and Ken Hodge.

"You just can't take anything away from them," Bobby Orr said. "Montreal made us play real bad."

Before leaving the Bruins' dressing room, Bobby remarked, "It's going to be a long, hot summer."

In this series, Bobby Orr was the first defense man in history to score a hat trick in a playoff game.

Dryden faced a puck barrage of 262 shots in the seven-game series from a team of Bruins sharpshooters. Boston had four men with 100-plus points and the all-time scoring leader in Espo with 76 goals and 152 points. The Bruins made shambles of the record books in the regular season but missed out on the Cup.

Weep not for the Bruins, though, for they shall return another day, with another Stanley Cup.

Crowd in Garden second balcony can't believe their eyes as the Bruins lose to Montreal in 1971 playoffs.

Time runs out on the Bruins.

A dejected Phil Esposito after 1971 series.

Bobby Orr wins two trophies

NHL awards also go to Phil Esposito and John Bucyk.

Boston's record-shattering Bruins, led by superstar Bobby Orr, captured four of the six individual NHL trophies in voting by members of the Professional Hockey Writers Association. Orr won two trophies—the Hart, his second straight, as most valuable player; and the Norris, his fourth, as best NHL defense man.

Bobby Orr and Eddie Shore are the only defense men in history to be named MVP twice. He tied the former Montreal great Doug Harvey in winning four consecutive Norris trophies.

Phil Esposito won the Art Ross Trophy as scoring champion for the second time in three years, and John Bucyk won the Lady Byng Trophy for combining sportsmanship with effective play.

Orr was the second-highest scorer in the league with 139 points, including a record 102 assists. He won the scoring title with 120 points in 1969–70.

In the Hart Trophy balloting, Orr had 151 points to 127 for Phil Esposito.

Bucyk, who finished third in scoring with 51 goals and 116 points, topped the Lady Byng voting with 166 points. Toronto's Dave Keon was next with 131. Bucyk had only eight minutes of penalties in the 1970–71 season.

Esposito, with his record-smashing 76 goals and 76 assists for 152 points, also won the Ross Trophy two seasons ago when he became the first man in NHL history to break the 100-point marker.

Each trophy brought a check for $1,500 to each Bruin.

Following page: *Orr gets ready to do his thing with the puck.*

149

Bruins win Stanley Cup over Rangers in New York

All agree Cup belongs to Bobby Orr.

"We're the champions," said Bobby Orr, and that just about tells the story of the Bruins' big Stanley Cup win over the New York Rangers.

Orr, winner of the Conn Smythe Trophy as the MVP in the playoffs, was swamped by hundreds of fans at Logan Airport as the Bruins' plane touched down in the early hours of the morning.

Bobby Orr scored a goal and assisted on another in the exciting grand finale at Madison Square Garden.

"New York has a hell of a hockey club, but we felt all along that we'd win," said Orr.

"That Orr, he's fantastic, just super," raved Brad Park, the NHL's number-two defense man, behind Boston's Number 4.

Vic Hadfield, Rangers captain, remarked, "You want to know what turned the game around for the Bruins? Bobby Orr. Our two clubs were even in everything—except one. The Bruins had Bobby Orr."

Orr was simply fantastic in the New York finale, even with a ten-minute misconduct for giving some lip to referee Art Skov. He did everything he usually does—blocking shots, checking, running the game like a quarterback—just a super show. Gerry Cheevers came up with a strong game in goal as he gained his second shutout of the playoffs.

A happy Bobby Orr and a happy Dallas Smith, with a happy Phil Esposito taking up the rear.

Bobby Orr takes a big swig from the cup of victory in New York after taking the Rangers apart in 1972.

"Give Cheesy the credit," said Orr. "He did a helluva job, especially in the second period. It was a nineteen-man job, with everybody working together—a real team effort."

Coach Tom Johnson took the kudos in stride. He was pleased as punch on the champagne flight back to Boston on the Eastern charter. "We beat a real good club," said Johnson. "Last year we ran out of gas in the playoffs, but not this year. This was the best all-around game we've played."

Orr's first goal was the game winner, the second time that an Orr goal had claimed a Stanley Cup. Only three players in the history of the NHL—Jean Beliveau, Henri Richard and Toe Blake, all of them Canadiens—have two Stanley Cup-winning goals to their credit.

Wayne Cashman scored twice for the Bruins, one on a deflected Orr screamer from the blue line on a Boston power play, the other on passes from Hodge and Espo in the last two minutes.

"It's always great when you win," Bobby Orr said after collecting both the Conn Smythe Trophy and its $1,500 prize, plus a new car for being judged the MVP in the Stanley Cup series.

May 11, 1972

Logan devastated by happy B's fans

Only a few of the Bruins struggled through the delirious crowd that started gathering at Logan Airport at midnight and waited until the Bruins' plane set down at 2:15 A.M.

After the first few players—Gerry Cheevers, Eddie Johnston and John McKenzie—were engulfed, Eastern Airlines officials decided to pull away the jet ramp and have the rest of the team take the chartered plane's stairs to the field. The first Bruins were pushed and pulled through the mob into the Eastern cocktail lounge.

A sign read, BRUINS REGAIN CUP, THANKS TO A GUY NAMED ORR.

"All you do is look up and see Number 4, and you know how it was done," said one fan.

"Orr dominated it, directed the whole thing. What a man, what a player!" exclaimed another.

Bobby Orr has been on two Stanley Cup teams and has won the final games in both series.

"Pick a man," Emile Francis said in New York, "on a team like the Bruins, and it's like picking the largest raindrop in the sky. They're good, excellent. But Orr, he's something else again. He's everything they say he is and even more. He's the guy who made us lose. Orr was the reason."

New York people were saying, "The Bruins have the secret ingredients for a hockey dynasty—Bobby Orr and Phil Esposito."

It might be good to do a little remembering about Bobby Orr in the 1972 playoffs.

Remember the great move Bobby put on Bruce MacGregor for the first goal, the winning tally.

Remember the great defensive work of Number 4.

Remember how he won the Conn Smythe Trophy twice in three years, the first player to be voted that honor twice.

Remember Clarence Campbell's statement, "Orr has everything: instinct, anticipation, ability and competitiveness."

Remember the 1970 Stanley Cup, but be sure to include Bobby Orr in your memories.

Preceding page: *1971–72 Boston Bruins, Stanley Cup champions.*
Front row: *Gerry Cheevers, John Bucyk, Phil Esposito, General Manager Milt Schmidt, Coach Tom Johnson, Eddie Westfall, Ted Green, Ed Johnston*
Middle row: *Trainer Dan Canney, Mike Walton, Garnet Bailey, Carol Vadnais, Don Awrey, Don Marcotte, Wayne Cashman, Assistant Trainer John Forristall*
Back row: *John McKenzie, Bobby Orr, Dallas Smith, Ken Hodge, Derek Sanderson, Fred Stanfield*

One player, McKenzie—one Cup, Stanley.

100,000 gather at City Hall Plaza to honor Stanley Cup champions

More than 100,000 shouting hockey fans paid tribute to the Boston Bruins—winners of their second Stanley Cup in three years—at City Hall Plaza. Before the world's greatest hockey team came into view on a City Hall balcony, they were honored at a private luncheon in Mayor Kevin White's office. And it was a merry old time in the Mayor of Boston's office.

In 1970, when Mayor White hosted a luncheon after the Bruins won the Stanley Cup, Johnny McKenzie dumped a bucket of beer suds over the mayor's head.

This time, Mayor White manned the bucket of beer. He gleefully gave McKenzie a malt-suds shampoo. The Bruins' Ken Hodge did a like job on State Treasurer Bob Crane, and Crane took care of Westy Adams, Jr., the Bruins' young president, with the beer that was left.

The Bruins received a thunderous ovation as they were introduced by Fred Cusick, the Bruins' TV voice. The biggest cheers were reserved for Bobby Orr, Wayne Cashman and Gerry Cheevers.

The crowd had started gathering in the Plaza around 8:30 A.M. and by noon had surpassed 100,000.

It was not a school holiday, but the huge throng contained thousands of school kids.

The Bruins' John Bucyk came to the mayor's buffet lugging the prized Stanley Cup.

"Where's the mayor?" yelled Orr when he breezed through the door. "Don't tell me Kevin's left town?"

Catching sight of Hodge holding a beer sign, Mayor White yelled, "Holy God, here we go again. Let's get out on the balcony."

The Bruins soon popped out on a City Hall balcony above a banner that read, THE PUCK STOPS HERE—CONGRATULATIONS, BRUINS. Wayne Cashman tossed his socks to the crowd, then his shirt, and then did his great imitation of Johnny Cash. The fans ate up Cash's version of the other Cash.

The noise was deafening as the tremendous crowd shouted, "We're number one! We're number one!"

The Bruins' assistant trainer, John "Frosty" Forristall, told the large gathering, "We're the greatest team ever to lace on skates, and the Boston fans are the greatest in the world." The crowd noisily agreed with his every word.

There was no parade as in 1970; none was really needed. It had all happened at Boston City Hall Plaza.

The PUCK STOPS HERE!

Bruins venture out to the balcony at City Hall.

Place: *City Hall Plaza, Boston.* Event: *A welcome to the 1972 Stanley Cup champions.*

October 1, 1972

Harry Sinden returns to the Bruins

After a two-year absence, Harry Sinden returned to the Bruins organization today as the club's managing director.

January 1973

Bep Guidolin replaces Johnson as coach

The former World War II Bruins player "Bep" Guidolin has taken over the team's coaching duties.

May 1973

Plante plants himself in Boston

Jacques Plante, the veteran goal tender, arrived in Boston in March, while the Bruins were sitting around in the league's quiet third spot.

Jacques Plante, 1972–73.

He won ten consecutive games, and the club finished the year in the higher second slot.

In the first round of the Stanley Cup, the Bruins were eliminated by the Rangers, thus getting the local team off to an early summer.

August 1973

Bruins merge with Storer

The Boston Garden-Arena Corporation and the Boston Bruins were merged into the Storer Broadcasting Corporation in a recently completed business arrangement.

Weston W. Adams, Jr., remains as president of both the Garden-Arena and the Boston Bruins.

◆◆◆◆◆◆

1973–74.

The Bruins won the Prince of Wales Trophy for scoring the most points in the entire NHL for the 1973–74 season.

In the Stanley Cup finals they lost to the Philadelphia Flyers four games to two, with the Flyers taking the fourth and deciding game 1–0 in Philadelphia, the cherished home of Bobby Clarke and Bernie Parent.

◆◆◆◆◆◆

June 1974

Don Cherry now coach

Last year Don Cherry coached in Rochester, New York. He has now been promoted to a top spot with the Boston Bruins as their new bench leader.

◆◆◆◆◆◆

1974–75.

This was the first season of the NHL's new divisional setup. Boston was placed in the Adams section, where they ended the year as runner-up to the strong Buffalo Sabres.

The Chicago Blackhawks eliminated the Bruins at Boston Garden in the first round of the Stanley Cup.

Bobby Orr won the scoring title, closely followed by another Bruin, Phil Esposito. Over the past few years these two have consistently been at the top of the lists in scoring and awards.

◆◆◆◆◆◆

BRUINS VS. DETROIT

JOHN BUCYK'S 1000TH POINT

NOV. 9, 1972

May 28, 1975

Espo and O'Reilly sign pacts

It was announced yesterday by the Bruins that Phil Esposito and Terry O'Reilly have been signed to "multi-year" contracts. Esposito said at the press conference, "I signed for two and a half times less than what the WHA offered." Phil went on, "I've been treated well in Boston and I'm very happy here."

No terms of the contracts were revealed, but both players seemed to be happy. More than likely, they're quite pleased with the financial arrangements for their next few years of hockey.

Harry Sinden announces Don Cherry as new Bruins coach for 1974–75.

Bobby Orr.

June 17, 1975

Orr wins again

Once again Bobby Orr has been announced as the winner of the Norris Trophy (best NHL defense man for 1974–75). This marks the eighth straight time that Orr has won the award, which is another great accomplishment for the Boston star.

No other trophy winner has ever walked off with any award eight times in a row, as Orr has done.

Bobby Orr has now added his sixteenth trophy to his vast collection. Earlier this month he was given the Art Ross Trophy for scoring the most points during the 1974–75 season. This was the second time that Orr has won the scoring title and the Ross Trophy.

In 1974–75 Orr had 46 goals and 89 assists for a league-leading total of 135 points.

Phil Esposito of the Bruins was runner-up with 61 goals and 66 assists for a total of 127 points.

Boston's Number 4 was also selected to this year's NHL All-Star team by a unanimous vote.

Orr tugs off jersey after another hard day's work.

August 28, 1975

Bruins sold for $10,000,000 to Buffalo group

The Boston Bruins and Boston Garden were sold today to Sportsystems Corporation of Buffalo, New York, an international firm employing more than 40,000 people in diversified services and products.

The National Hockey League Board of Governors, meeting in Toronto, approved the sale by the Storer Broadcasting Company for the reported sum of $10,000,000.

The Sportsystems group is headed by Buffalo businessman Jeremy Jacobs. His brother Max is a consultant with the firm. Another brother, Lawrence, is a neurologist.

Storer Broadcasting had purchased the Bruins and the Garden two years ago in a stock transaction that was figured to be around $16,000,000, with the real value estimated at about $7,200,000.

Bruins games will continue to be telecast by Storer's WSBK, Channel 38, under a long-term contract.

A Skate Back into Time:

Memorable statements from Bruins stars past and present

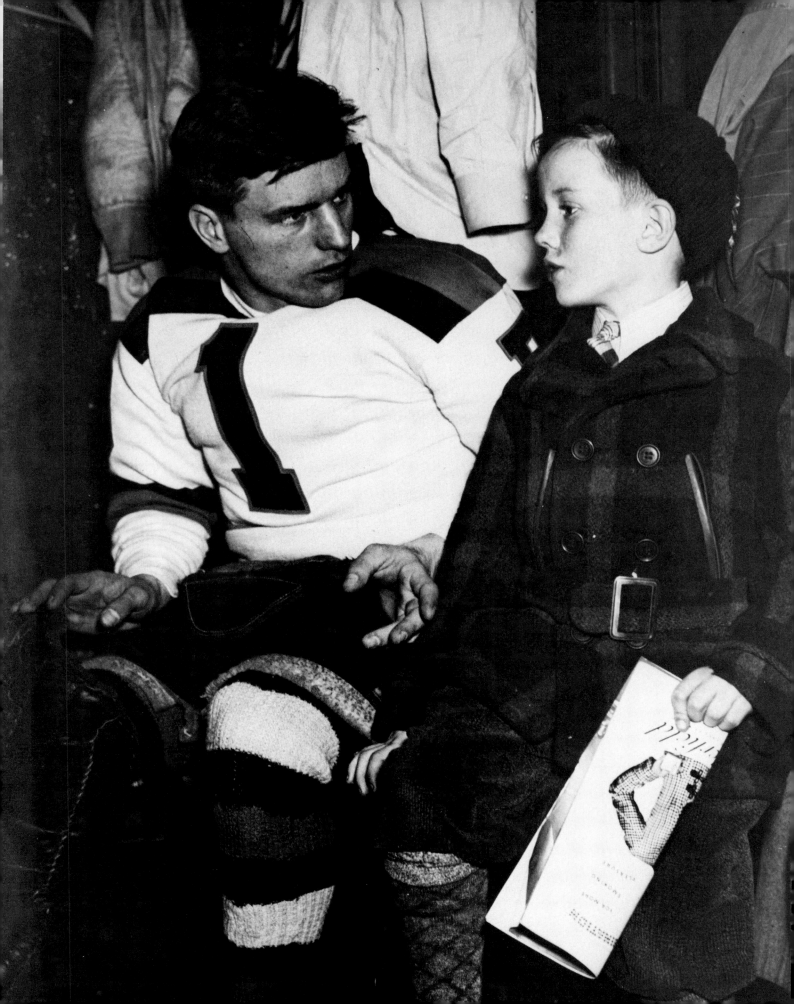

"I think making the Bruins back in the fall of 1938 has to be my fondest memory. I waited a long time for it. I'd played amateur in Pittsburgh and then in Baltimore. When I came east the last time with Baltimore, I had hopes I'd catch on with some pro team.

"Herb Mitchell, who coached Hershey in the old Eastern League, saw me playing for Baltimore against his team and recommended me to Art Ross, his old coach. Ross invited me to the Bruins' camp, but suddenly it was discovered that Detroit owned the rights to me and I had to go to the Detroit camp. I don't know how the Bruins wound up with my rights, but Detroit yelled 'robber' and the Bruins had to pay them some money.

"I played in Providence for a year, and then, when Tiny Thompson was hurt early in the fall of 1938, I was called up. It was the biggest moment of my life—here I was, finally in the big time."

Frank Brimsek

1938—1943, 1945—1949

"The worst day in my life was the day I left the Bruins. After twenty-two years as a player and coach, the Bruins were such a big part of my life. I'll never forget the wonderful bunch of guys with whom I was associated—Tiny Thompson, Eddie Shore, Marty Barry, Bill Cowley and the Krauts, Milt Schmidt, Bobby Bauer and Woody Dumart, to mention only a few. One of the big thrills of my career was playing right wing for Milt and Woody when they first came into the NHL. But they didn't need me very long. They were great. I always liked Art Ross, my coach and close friend, and I can't forget Weston Adams, either. He treated me fine in Boston."

Dit Clapper

1927—1947

"What I remember most is my back checking against Neil Colville in the 1939 Rangers playoffs. Colville broke away and I was the only one back—nobody believes this because I wasn't used to being a back checker—but I was the only one there, and I chased Colville, yelling at him all the time. I didn't know what to do, not being a good checker.

"When Art Ross and Cooney [Weiland], sitting next to each other on the bench, saw Colville going in alone on Brimsek and me alone there with him, they ducked under the boards, expecting the worst, and in the excitement banged their heads together. He [Colville] pulled Brimsek out of goal but shot wide and missed.

"This was only the second time I had ever back checked, and we won that game with a Mel Hill goal.

"The other time I back checked was in a game with the Montreal Maroons. Two Montreal players, Baldy Northcott and Lionel Conacher, raced in on Tiny Thompson in goal. I was the closest to them. Tiny shouted for me to take Northcott and he would handle Conacher, who had the puck. Conacher shot and didn't score.

"I had a one-hundred-percent record: two back checks in my career, and no goals scored."

Bill Cowley

1935—1947

"Every athlete wants to play on a championship team. I had the privilege of playing on two of the Bruins' Stanley Cup teams, in 1939 and 1941. Those were experiences I'll never forget, particularly in '39, the first Bruins' Cup victory in ten years. After we won the Cup on Garden ice against Toronto, the crowd's chanting a deafening, 'We want Shore,' was unforgettable.

"I'll also remember forever things like the night the fans gave us in January 1942 when Milt [Schmidt] and Bobby [Bauer] left for the service. We walloped the Canadiens that night, and the three of us had a barrel of points. I remember, too, the reception we received from the fans when we returned to the Bruins after our war service. Another big time was the night the fans gave Milt and I in 1952 when Bobby returned to play with us for that one night; and of course, the night I scored my two hundredth goal against Harry Lumley and Chicago at the Garden. I wasn't playing much at that time because it was near the end of my career, and I scored the goal using a brand new stick. It's probably the newest stick for a big goal in the Hockey Hall of Fame."

Woody Dumart

1936—1942, 1945—1954

"My eight seasons as a member of the Boston Bruins have been tremendously rewarding—for any number of reasons.

"But if I had to pick one individual thrill, I think it would be the night I scored my ninety-ninth point to set a National Hockey League record. It came during the 1968–69 season against the New York Rangers. We were short-handed at that time, and I took a pass from Ken Hodge and shot the puck under Ed Giacomin.

"The whole team came off the bench, and the crowd went wild. I'd never had anything like it happen to me before, and I was just thrilled. I still have the films of it, and they are very valuable to me.

"Of course, winning the Stanley Cup—especially the first time —is a tremendous thrill for any individual and team. Playing on two Cup teams thus far is great, and I hope I'll be on a few more before my playing career comes to an end.

"Being a member of the Bruins has been great, for sure. Just playing in the city of Boston is a big reason. It's a tremendous place to live and work.

"The Boston fans have been very classy as well. I remember the day that Bobby Hull walked through the crowd, headed for the television box, and got a standing ovation. And the night Gump Worsley got a standing O, and the night my brother Tony was pulled from a game and got a standing O, and on, and on. . . .

"They've been great years in Boston. I only hope they continue and we can work as a team to continue to give this city a championship hockey team."

Phil Esposito

1967—

"There's no way to condense nine years of thrills and highlights into just a few paragraphs, nor is it possible to select one moment as the most satisfying of all.

"But people say the first championship is always an athlete's most memorable experience, and I think I'd have to go along with that. Someone took an award-winning photograph of me sailing through the air just after I'd scored the overtime goal which gave the Bruins the 1970 Stanley Cup. But I'll never have to look at that picture to recall the total sense of joy I felt watching the puck skip over the crease. A lot of thoughts can flash through your mind in an instant like that; for me, it was the immediate culmination of a lifetime spent in hockey, an exhilarating feeling of having reached the very top of the mountain. Like millions of other young kids growing up in Canada, I dreamed of someday playing in the NHL. Now I was not only playing there; I was participating in its most cherished ceremony—capturing the Stanley Cup and having my name inscribed on it.

"If I played one thousand seasons and missed that experience, my career would be incomplete. That's how much the Stanley Cup means.

"And that's exactly what I was thinking as I sailed through the air at Boston Garden that fantastic afternoon."

Bobby Orr

1966—

"I'll never forget the night we were on our way to Toronto. We used to ride trains in those days in the fifties. The train stopped in Syracuse, and, as we customarily did, we strolled into the station to stretch our legs and get a paper or something to eat. Chevvy [Real Chevrefils] and Leo [Leo LaBine] were in pajamas, with just a pair of slacks and slippers. They announced that our train was about to leave, and we all ran back to the trains. Somehow Chevvy and LaBine got on the wrong train, and as ours pulled out we saw them at the window of the other train with the doggonedest expressions on their faces as they saw the rest of us sitting in the other train. Fortunately for them, their train was also going to Rochester, which was our next stop, and they joined us there. We had a barrel of laughs with them.

"Of all the things that happened during my years with the Bruins, I think the most exciting was the '53 playoffs, when we upset Detroit. The Red Wings had won more points than anybody else had ever won in a season up to then, and we had just made the playoffs. We lost the first game 7–0, and it looked bad. But we had our 'shadows,' Woody Dumart and Joe Klukay, covering Gordie Howe and Ted Lindsay so that they couldn't do a thing. I played on a line with Fleming Mackell and Ed Sandford, and we were the high scorers in the six-game series victory."

John Peirson

1946—1954, 1955—1958

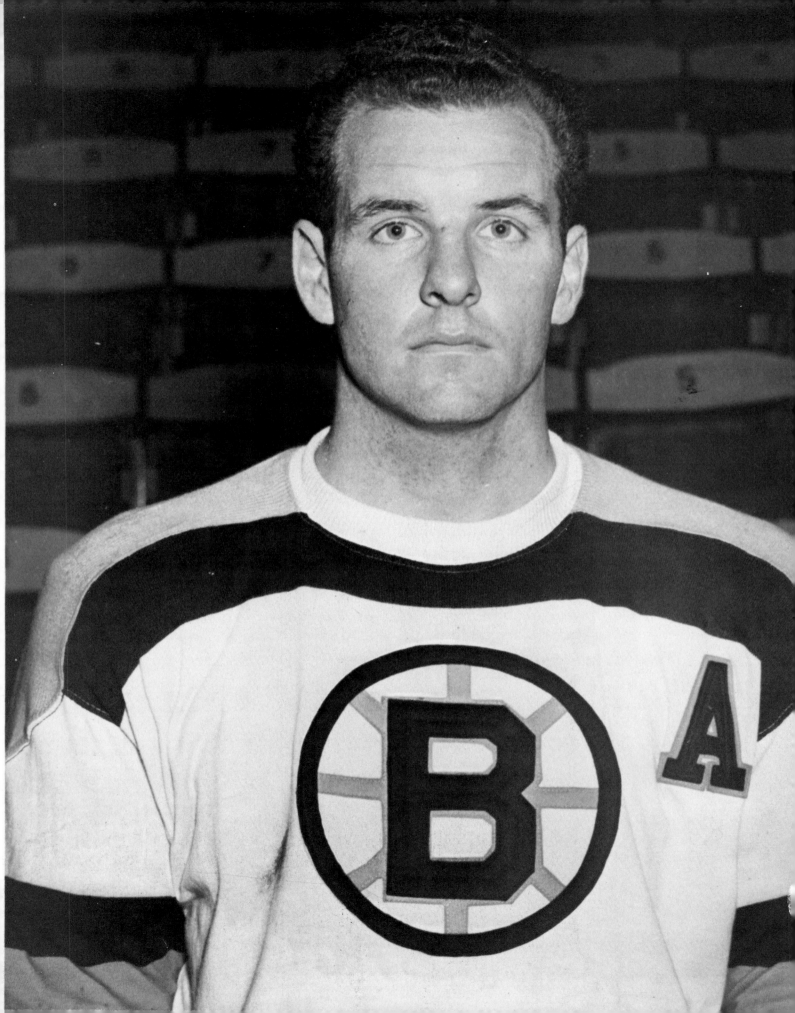

"I think going to camp with the Bruins for the first time was something I'll always remember. I was fresh out of junior hockey, and meeting Milt Schmidt, who was the Shore or Orr of his day, whichever way you want to put it, was a big thing to me. He was the best all-around forward of that era, in my opinion, and he was my idol. After I met him, I found him to be just what I expected— a great guy as well as a great player.

"My biggest thrill in hockey was upsetting Detroit in the 1953 series. We weren't supposed to have a chance against Ted Lindsay and Gordie Howe and Terry Sawchuk. They beat us in the first game 7–0. But we used the 'shadows,' Woody Dumart on Howe and Joe Klukay on Lindsay, with adjustments after that first game, and we beat them in six games."

Ed Sandford

1947—1955

"There are two things I remember most about my hockey career. The first was back in the fall of 1935, when the Bruins invited me to training camp at St. John's, Quebec. I wouldn't sign a contract with them that year, but they wanted me to come back again the following year, and when I left camp they gave me a brand new pair of skates. It was the first new pair I had ever had, and was I excited.

"The other big thrill was winning the Stanley Cup in 1939 and hearing the ovation the fans gave Eddie Shore. They wouldn't let the league president, Frank Calder, present the Stanley Cup to the Bruins until Shore, who had gone right into the dressing room at the final buzzer, returned to the ice."

Milt Schmidt

1936—1942, 1946—1955

"We were playing the Canadiens in a pre-season game back in the thirties, and even though it was just an exhibition game we were checking hard. I caught one of their defense men, Jean Pusie, with one of the hardest checks I ever threw. He went down as I skated away, and along came Dit Clapper. As Dit skated past, Pusie looked up at him and said, 'You can't do that to me.'

"My greatest thrill? I'd have to say the ovation the fans gave me the night we beat Toronto at the Garden for the Stanley Cup in 1939."

Eddie Shore

1926—1940

"I must state I have always respected and appreciated the enthusiasm and sincerity of the Boston fans.

"Probably my biggest thrill was the club's winning the Stanley Cup in my rookie year.

"As for former players, the defense men Hitchman and Shore together made a great defense, as their different styles of play complemented each other.

"The forward line most remembered was that of Clapper, Gainor and Weiland in the early thirties, because for two years they were the greatest.

"The biggest disappointment was the 1–0 loss to Toronto in that long overtime playoff game, which should have been a victory for us on a disallowed goal in regular time.

"Naturally, I was disappointed in my trade to Detroit, but this was expected because of Brimsek's ability and the big difference in age."

Tiny Thompson

1928—1939

"I was at the Garden one night scouting the Bruins and Pittsburgh for the Los Angeles Kings. Phil Esposito scored a goal, and the public address announcer said it was his forty-sixth of the season. I thought to myself, Good gosh, I didn't score that many in three seasons, let alone one!

"But hockey to us was a lot of fun. Maybe we enjoyed it more those days than the players do today, even if we didn't make as much money."

Jerry Toppazzini

1952—1954, 1955—1964

"When I look back over the years and reminisce about hockey, I always think about my first year with the Bruins in 1928–29. We won the Stanley Cup, the first ever for the Bruins. It was a great thrill for a rookie like me and for our goal tender, Tiny Thompson. I scored the winning goal in each of the first two games of the semi-final series against the Montreal Canadiens, both 1–0 games. We beat the Rangers for the Cup in the finale.

"Another fond memory was winning the Stanley Cup as a coach in 1941.

"You have your high points and you have your low ones. I'd have to say that my big disappointment was in 1929–30, when we lost only five games all season and I led the league in scoring with forty-four goals and seventy-seven points, and yet we lost out in the playoffs to the Canadiens in the first round."

Cooney Weiland

1928—1932, 1935—1939

Art Ross, 1924–25—1933–34; 1936–37—1938–39; 1941–42.

Frank Patrick, 1934–35—1935–36.

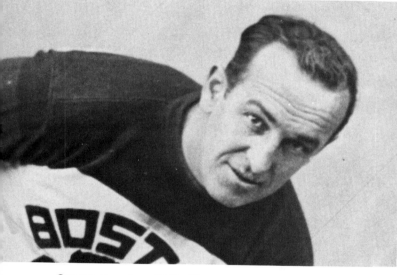

George Boucher, 1949–50.

Lynn Patrick, 1950–51—1954–55.

Harry Sinden, 1966–67—1969–70.

Tom Johnson, 1970–71—1972–73.

Bruins

Cooney Weiland, 1939–40—1940–41.

Dit Clapper, 1942–43—1948–49.

Milt Schmidt, 1954–55—1960–61; 1962–63—1965–66.

Phil Watson, 1961–62—1962–63.

Bep Guidolin, 1972–73—1973–74.

Don Cherry, 1974–75—

Coaches

Bruins in
Black and White

Boston Garden in 1930.

Ted Green mixes with Brad Park of the Rangers, as the referee keeps out of harm's way.

Preceding page: *Both benches, Bruins and Canadiens, are emptied as teams tangle all over the place.*

Bobby Orr.

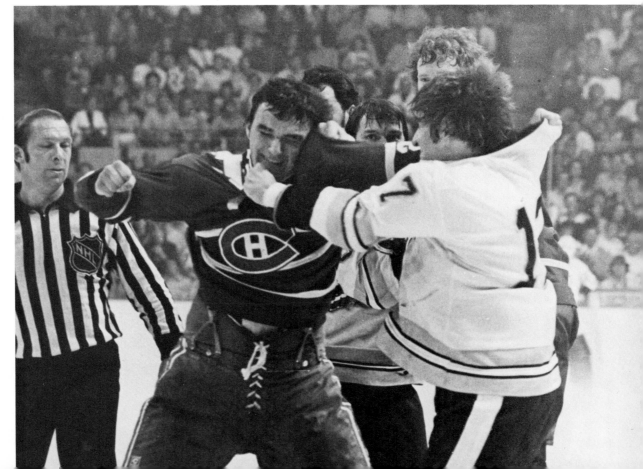

Bob Schmautz seems upset with a man from Montreal.

Eddie Shore.

Preceding page: *Inside the Garden, the quaint home of the Bruins.*

198

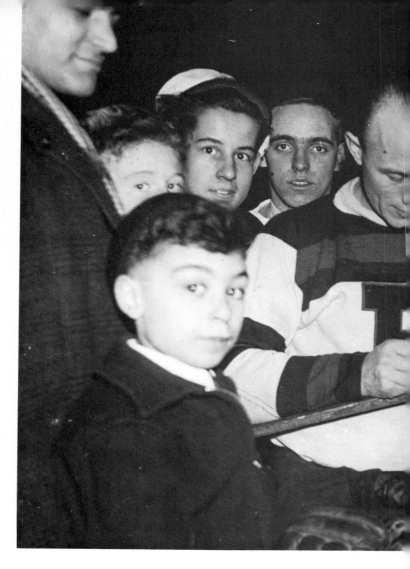

Every red-blooded kid wanted an Eddie Shore autograph.

Senior citizen Eddie Shore.

Eddie Shore and Ace Bailey in 1970, gazing at the Lester Patrick Trophy that Shore had won for his outstanding service to hockey in the United States. This was thirty-seven years after the famous Shore-Bailey incident in Boston.

Old-timers return to Boston for special night on ice in late 1960s. Back row: *Dit Clapper, Frank Brimsek, Woody Dumart, Cooney Weiland.* Front row: *Milt Schmidt and Eddie Wiseman.*

Some of the boys before a 1935 away game taking it easy in their luxurious hotel suite: *Dit Clapper, Marty Barry, Tiny Thompson and Max Kaminsky.*

Weston Adams, Jr., Bobby Orr and Alan Eagleson
enjoying a Boston press meeting.

Art Ross chatting with Hooley Smith, left, and Allan Shields
about their social life. The year is 1937.

A quiet 1965 Bruins dressing room, with Hap Emms talking softly with Milt Schmidt—another game lost in one of the tough years of the early sixties. But things would start looking up—Bobby Orr was just coming around the corner.

Preceding page: *Sunday night at Boston Garden in 1975.*

Lionel Hitchman playing the part of hockey's Robin Hood with his trusted bow and arrows.

Center, top: *Nels Stewart and his wife enjoying an evening at home in 1936.*

Bottom: *Trainer Dan Canney hangs up the super number 4 in the dressing room.*

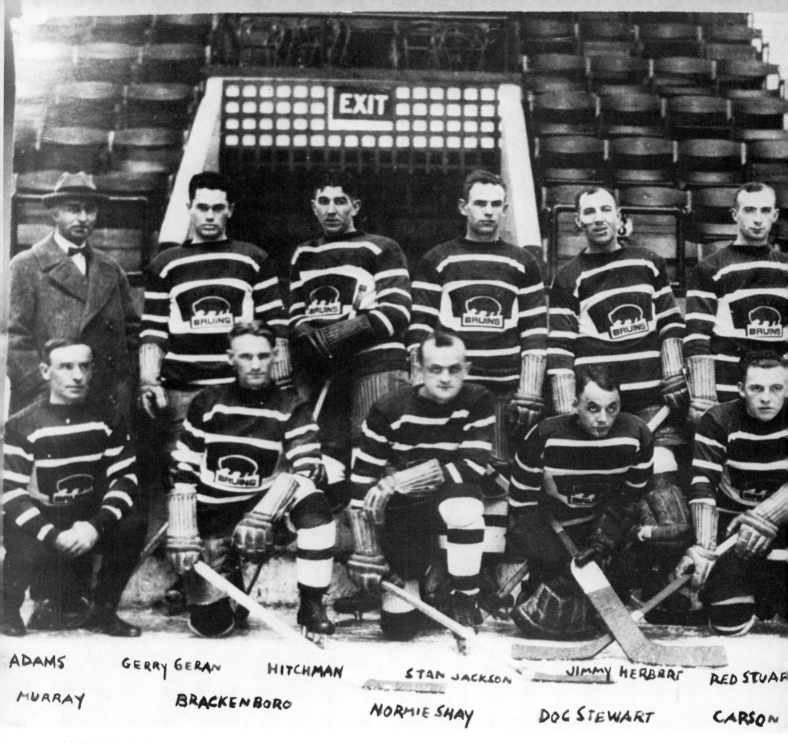

ADAMS   GERRY GERAN   HITCHMAN   STAN JACKSON   JIMMY HERBERT   RED STUART

MURRAY   BRACKENBORO   NORMIE SHAY   DOC STEWART   CARSON

1925-26 Bruins team.

Preceding page: *Montreal vs. Bruins in 1970
misunderstanding at Boston Garden.*

208

TEAM-LEADING SCORERS

	Points	Goals	Assists	Penalties Minutes
1924-25	22 J. Herberts	17 J. Herberts	5 J. Herberts	50 J. Herberts
1925-26	31 C. Cooper J. Herberts	28 C. Cooper	5 S. Cleghorn J. Herberts	70 L. Hitchman
1926-27	31 F. Fredrickson	18 F. Fredrickson H. Oliver	13 F. Fredrickson	130 E. Shore
1927-28	18 H. Oliver	13 H. Oliver	6 E. Shore	165 E. Shore
1928-29	23 H. Oliver	17 H. Oliver	8 W. Carson	96 E. Shore
1929-30	73 C. Weiland	43 C. Weiland	31 N. Gainor	105 E. Shore
1930-31	38 C. Weiland	25 C. Weiland	16 E. Shore	105 E. Shore
1931-32	39 A. Clapper	21 M. Barry	22 A. Clapper	80 E. Shore
1932-33	37 M. Barry	24 M. Barry	27 E. Shore	102 E. Shore
1933-34	39 M. Barry	27 M. Barry	17 N. Stewart	68 N. Stewart
1934-35	40 M. Barry	21 A. Clapper N. Stewart	26 E. Shore	80 A. Siebert
1935-36	32 J. Beattie	14 J. Beattie	18 J. Beattie	66 A. Siebert
1936-37	35 W. Cowley	18 C. Sands	22 W. Cowley	94 A. Shields
1937-38	39 W. Cowley	20 R. Bauer	22 W. Cowley	54 W. Hollett
1938-39	42 W. Cowley	26 R. Conacher	34 W. Cowley	47 E. Shore
1939-40	52 M. Schmidt	22 M. Schmidt W. Dumart	30 M. Schmidt	55 J. Shewchuk
1940-41	62 W. Cowley	24 R. Conacher	45 W. Cowley	61 D. Smith
1941-42	37 R. Conacher	24 R. Conacher	23 W. Cowley	70 D. Smith
1942-43	72 W. Cowley	27 W. Cowley	45 W. Cowley	67 M. Chamberlain
1943-44	82 H. Cain	36 H. Cain	46 H. Cain	75 P. Egan
1944-45	65 W. Cowley	32 H. Cain	40 W. Cowley	86 P. Egan
1945-46	40 D. Gallinger	22 W. Dumart	23 D. Gallinger	62 A. Guidolin
1946-47	62 M. Schmidt	30 R. Bauer	35 M. Schmidt	89 P. Egan
1947-48	40 G. Warwick	23 G. Warwick P. Babando	23 K. Smith	81 P. Egan
1948-49	49 P. Ronty	22 J. Peirson G. Warwick	29 P. Ronty	92 P. Egan
1949-50	59 P. Ronty	27 J. Peirson	36 P. Ronty	122 F. Flaman
1950-51	61 M. Schmidt	22 M. Schmidt	39 M. Schmidt	119 W. Ezinicki
1951-52	50 M. Schmidt J. Peirson	21 M. Schmidt	30 J. Peirson	127 W. Kyle
1952-53	44 F. Mackell	27 F. Mackell	23 M. Schmidt	69 L. LaBine
1953-54	47 F. Mackell E. Sandford	21 J. Peirson	32 F. Mackell	81 R. Armstrong
1954-55	42 L. LaBine D. McKenney	24 L. LaBine	24 F. Mackell	150 F. Flaman
1955-56	37 V. Stasiuk	19 V. Stasiuk	24 D. McKenney	122 R. Armstrong
1956-57	60 D. McKenney	31 R. Chevrefils	39 D. McKenney	128 L. LaBine
1957-58	66 B. Horvath	30 B. Horvath	40 F. Mackell	72 F. Mackell
1958-59	62 D. McKenney	32 D. McKenney	36 J. Bucyk	101 F. Flaman
1959-60	80 B. Horvath	39 B. Horvath	49 D. McKenney	121 V. Stasiuk
1960-61	50 G. Toppazzini	26 D. McKenney	35 G. Toppazzini	95 J. Bartlett
1961-62	60 J. Bucyk	22 D. McKenney	40 J. Bucyk	116 T. Green
1962-63	66 J. Bucyk	27 J. Bucyk	40 M. Oliver	117 T. Green
1963-64	68 M. Oliver	24 M. Oliver	44 M. Oliver	145 T. Green
1964-65	55 J. Bucyk	26 J. Bucyk	29 J. Bucyk	156 T. Green
1965-66	60 M. Oliver	27 J. Bucyk	42 M. Oliver	113 T. Green
1966-67	48 J. Bucyk	20 H. Martin	30 J. Bucyk	112 G. Marotte
1967-68	84 P. Esposito	35 P. Esposito	49 P. Esposito	150 D. Awrey
1968-69	126 P. Esposito	49 P. Esposito	77 P. Esposito	146 D. Sanderson
1969-70	120 R. Orr	43 P. Esposito	87 R. Orr	125 R. Orr
1970-71	152 P. Esposito	76 P. Esposito	102 R. Orr	141 D. Awrey
1971-72	133 P. Esposito	66 P. Esposito	80 R. Orr	132 D. Smith
1972-73	130 P. Esposito	55 P. Esposito	75 P. Esposito	127 C. Vadnais
1973-74	145 P. Esposito	68 P. Esposito	90 R. Orr	123 C. Vadnais
1974-75	135 R. Orr	61 P. Esposito	89 R. Orr	146 T. O'Reilly

Preceding page: *Dit Clapper has a few choice words with Phil Watson of the New York Rangers in 1939.*

Individual and
Team Records

RB MITCHELL A. ROSS

GEO. REDDING

Boston's McKenzie and Chicago's Magnuson get ready to have a go.

BRUINS ALL-TIME RECORDS

Season	Won	Lost	Tied	Points	Goals For	Goals Agst.	Finished Position
1924-25	6	24	0	12	49	119	Sixth (6)
1925-26	17	15	4	38	92	85	Fourth (7)
1926-27	21	20	3	45	97	89	Second (AD)
1927-28	20	13	11	51	77	70	First (AD)
1928-29	26	13	5	57	89	52	*First (AD)
1929-30	38	5	1	77	179	98	First (AD)
1930-31	28	10	6	62	143	90	First (AD)
1931-32	15	21	12	42	122	117	Fourth (AD)
1932-33	25	15	8	58	124	88	First (AD)
1933-34	18	25	5	41	111	130	Fourth (AD)
1934-35	26	16	6	58	129	112	First (AD)
1935-36	22	20	6	50	92	83	Second (AD)
1936-37	23	18	7	53	120	110	Second (AD)
1937-38	30	11	7	67	142	89	First (AD)
1938-39	36	10	2	74	156	76	*First (7)
1939-40	31	12	5	67	170	98	First (7)
1940-41	27	8	13	67	168	102	*First (7)
1941-42	25	17	6	56	160	118	Third (7)
1942-43	24	17	9	57	195	176	Second (6)
1943-44	19	26	5	43	223	268	Fifth (6)
1944-45	16	30	4	36	179	219	Fourth (6)
1945-46	24	18	8	56	167	156	Second (6)
1946-47	26	23	11	63	190	175	Third (6)
1947-48	23	24	13	59	167	168	Third (6)
1948-49	29	23	8	66	178	163	Second (6)
1949-50	22	32	16	60	198	228	Fifth (6)
1950-51	22	30	18	62	178	197	Fourth (6)
1951-52	25	29	16	66	162	176	Fourth (6)
1952-53	28	29	13	69	152	172	Third (6)
1953-54	32	28	10	74	177	181	Fourth (6)
1954-55	23	26	21	67	169	188	Fourth (6)
1955-56	23	34	13	59	147	185	Fifth (6)
1956-57	34	24	12	80	195	174	Third (6)
1957-58	27	28	15	69	199	194	Fourth (6)
1958-59	32	29	9	73	205	215	Second (6)
1959-60	28	34	8	64	220	241	Fifth (6)
1960-61	15	42	13	43	176	254	Sixth (6)
1961-62	15	47	8	38	177	306	Sixth (6)
1962-63	14	39	17	45	198	281	Sixth (6)
1963-64	18	40	12	48	170	212	Sixth (6)
1964-65	21	43	6	48	166	253	Sixth (6)
1965-66	21	43	6	48	174	275	Fifth (6)
1966-67	17	43	10	44	182	253	Sixth (6)
1967-68	37	27	10	84	259	215	Third (ED)
1968-69	42	18	16	100	303	221	Second (ED)
1969-70	40	17	19	99	277	216	*Second (ED)
1970-71	57	14	7	121	399	207	First (ED)
1971-72	54	13	11	119	330	204	*First (ED)
1972-73	51	22	5	107	330	235	Second (ED)
1973-74	52	17	9	113	349	221	First (ED)
1974-75	40	26	14	94	345	245	Second **(AD)

*Won Stanley Cup.   ( ) Teams in league.   (AD) American Division
(ED) Eastern Division   **(AD) Adams Division

ACTIVE 20-GOAL BRUINS

76 **Phil Esposito, 1970-71**
68 Phil Esposito, 1973-74
66 Phil Esposito, 1971-72
61 Phil Esposito, 1974-75
55 Phil Esposito, 1972-73
49 Phil Esposito, 1968-69
43 Phil Esposito, 1969-70
35 Phil Esposito, 1967-68

51 **John Bucyk, 1970-71**
40 John Bucyk, 1972-73
32 John Bucyk, 1971-72
31 John Bucyk, 1973-74
31 John Bucyk, 1969-70
30 John Bucyk, 1967-68
29 John Bucyk, 1974-75
27 John Bucyk, 1965-66
27 John Bucyk, 1962-63
26 John Bucyk, 1964-65
24 John Bucyk, 1968-69
24 John Bucyk, 1958-59
21 John Bucyk, 1957-58
20 John Bucyk, 1961-62

50 **Ken Hodge, 1973-74**
45 Ken Hodge, 1968-69

43 Ken Hodge, 1970-71
37 Ken Hodge, 1972-73
25 Ken Hodge, 1967-68
25 Ken Hodge, 1969-70
23 Ken Hodge, 1974-75

46 **Bobby Orr, 1974-75**
37 Bobby Orr, 1970-71
37 Bobby Orr, 1971-72
33 Bobby Orr, 1969-70
32 Bobby Orr, 1973-74
29 Bobby Orr, 1972-73
21 Bobby Orr, 1968-69

30 **Wayne Cashman, 1973-74**
29 Wayne Cashman, 1972-73
23 Wayne Cashman, 1971-72
21 Wayne Cashman, 1970-71

31 **Don Marcotte, 1974-75**
24 Don Marcotte, 1972-73
24 Don Marcotte, 1973-74

30 **Gregg Sheppard, 1974-75**
24 Gregg Sheppard, 1972-73

21 **Bobby Schmautz, 1974-75**

TROPHY WINNERS

Georges Vezina Trophy—for goal tender with best record:

1929-30 Cecil (Tiny) Thompson	1937-38 Cecil (Tiny) Thompson
1932-33 Cecil (Tiny) Thompson	1938-39 Frank Brimsek
1935-36 Cecil (Tiny) Thompson	1941-42 Frank Brimsek

Dr. David A. Hart Trophy—for most valuable player:

1932-33 Eddie Shore	1950-51 Milton Schmidt
1934-35 Eddie Shore	1968-69 Phil Esposito
1935-36 Eddie Shore	1969-70 Bobby Orr
1937-38 Eddie Shore	1970-71 Bobby Orr
1940-41 Bill Cowley	1971-72 Bobby Orr
1942-43 Bill Cowley	1973-74 Phil Esposito

Lady Byng Trophy—for most gentlemanly player:

1939-40 Bobby Bauer	1959-60 Don McKenney
1940-41 Bobby Bauer	1970-71 John Bucyk
1946-47 Bobby Bauer	1973-74 John Bucyk

Calder Trophy—for outstanding rookie:

1938-39 Frank Brimsek	1966-67 Bobby Orr
1949-50 Jack Gelineau	1967-68 Derek Sanderson
1956-57 Larry Regan	

James Norris Memorial Trophy—for outstanding defense man:

1967-68 Bobby Orr	1971-72 Bobby Orr
1968-69 Bobby Orr	1972-73 Bobby Orr
1969-70 Bobby Orr	1973-74 Bobby Orr
1970-71 Bobby Orr	1974-75 Bobby Orr

Art Ross Trophy—for scoring leader:

1929-30 Cooney Weiland	1970-71 Phil Esposito
1939-40 Milt Schmidt	1971-72 Phil Esposito
1940-41 Bill Cowley	1972-73 Phil Esposito
1943-44 Herb Cain	1973-74 Phil Esposito
1968-69 Phil Esposito	1974-75 Bobby Orr
1969-70 Bobby Orr	

Conn Smythe Trophy—most valuable player to team in playoffs:
1969-70 Bobby Orr
1971-72 Bobby Orr

Lester Patrick Trophy—outstanding service to hockey in the
United States
1967 Charles F. Adams
1968 Walter A. Brown
1970 Eddie Shore
1972 Cooney Weiland
1974 Weston W. Adams, Sr.

TOP SCORERS—LIFETIME

(Scoring for Bruins only)

No.	Player	Regular Season					Playoffs				
		GP	G	A	Pts	PIM	GP	G	A	Pts	PIM
1.	John Bucyk	1257	484	711	1195	400	92	38	52	90	34
2.	Phil Esposito	613	453	543	996	504	71	46	56	102	86
3.	Bobby Orr	621	259	611	870	902	74	26	66	92	107
4.	Ken Hodge	580	264	349	613	578	74	30	41	71	104
5.	Milt Schmidt	776	229	346	575	466	86	24	25	49	60
6.	Bill Cowley		190	348	538	112	62	12	34	46	22
7.	Dit Clapper	830	228	246	474	252	81	13	17	30	46
8.	Don McKenney	592	195	267	462	189	34	13	20	33	8
9.	Woody Dumart	771	211	218	429	99	82	12	15	27	23
10.	Fred Stanfield	448	135	274	409	80	55	17	29	46	6

LEAGUE-LEADING SCORERS

	Year	Games	Gls.	Assts.	Pts.	Pen.
Cooney Weiland	1929-30	44	43	30	73	27
Milt Schmidt	1939-40	48	22	30	52	37
Bill Cowley	1940-41	48	17	45	62	16
Herb Cain	1943-44	48	36	46	82	4
Phil Esposito	1968-69	76	49	77	126	79
Bobby Orr	1969-70	76	33	87	120	125
Phil Esposito	1970-71	78	76	76	152	71
Phil Esposito	1971-72	76	66	67	133	76
Phil Esposito	1972-73	78	55	75	130	87
Phil Esposito	1973-74	78	68	77	145	58
Bobby Orr	1974-75	80	46	89	135	101

STANLEY CUP RECORD

Season	Opponent	Won	Lost	Tied	Goals For	Agst.	Winner
1924-25	Did not qualify						Victoria Cougars
1925-26	Did not qualify						Montreal Maroons
1926-27	Chicago	1	0	1	10	5	
	Rangers	1	0	1	3	1	
	Ottawa	0	2	2	3	7	Ottawa Senators
1927-28	Rangers	0	1	1	2	5	New York Rangers
1928-29	Canadiens	3	0	0	5	2	
	Rangers	2	0	0	4	1	BOSTON BRUINS
1929-30	Maroons	3	1	0	11	5	
	Canadiens	0	2	0	3	7	Montreal Canadiens
1930-31	Canadiens	2	3	0	13	13	Montreal Canadiens
1931-32	Did not qualify						Toronto Maple Leafs
1932-33	Toronto	2	3	0	7	9	New York Rangers
1933-34	Did not qualify						Chicago Blackhawks
1934-35	Toronto	1	3	0	2	7	Montreal Maroons
1935-36	Toronto	1	1	0	6	8	Detroit Red Wings
1936-37	Maroons	1	2	0	6	8	Detroit Red Wings
1937-38	Toronto	0	3	0	3	6	Chicago Blackhawks
1938-39	Rangers	4	3	0	14	12	
	Toronto	4	1	0	12	6	BOSTON BRUINS
1939-40	Rangers	2	4	0	9	15	New York Rangers
1940-41	Toronto	4	3	0	15	17	
	Detroit	4	0	0	12	6	BOSTON BRUINS
1941-42	Chicago	2	1	0	5	7	
	Detroit	0	2	0	5	9	Toronto Maple Leafs
1942-43	Canadiens	4	1	0	18	17	
	Detroit	0	4	0	5	16	Detroit Red Wings
1943-44	Did not qualify						Montreal Canadiens
1944-45	Detroit	3	4	0	22	22	Toronto Maple Leafs
1945-46	Detroit	4	1	0	16	10	
	Canadiens	1	4	0	13	19	Montreal Canadiens
1946-47	Canadiens	1	4	0	10	16	Toronto Maple Leafs
1947-48	Toronto	1	4	0	13	20	Toronto Maple Leafs
1948-49	Toronto	1	4	0	10	16	Toronto Maple Leafs
1949-50	Did not qualify						Detroit Red Wings
1950-51	Toronto	1	4	1	5	17	Toronto Maple Leafs
1951-52	Canadiens	3	4	0	12	18	Detroit Red Wings
1952-53	Detroit	4	2	0	21	21	
	Canadiens	1	4	0	9	16	Montreal Canadiens
1953-54	Canadiens	0	4	0	4	16	Detroit Red Wings
1954-55	Canadiens	1	4	0	9	16	Detroit Red Wings
1955-56	Did not qualify						Montreal Canadiens
1956-57	Detroit	4	1	0	15	14	
	Canadiens	1	4	0	6	15	Montreal Canadiens
1957-58	Rangers	4	2	0	28	16	
	Canadiens	2	4	0	14	16	Montreal Canadiens
1958-59	Toronto	3	4	0	21	20	Montreal Canadiens
1959-60	Did not qualify						Montreal Canadiens
1960-61	Did not qualify						Chicago Blackhawks
1961-62	Did not qualify						Toronto Maple Leafs
1962-63	Did not qualify						Toronto Maple Leafs
1963-64	Did not qualify						Toronto Maple Leafs
1964-65	Did not qualify						Montreal Canadiens
1965-66	Did not qualify						Montreal Canadiens
1966-67	Did not qualify						Toronto Maple Leafs
1967-68	Canadiens	0	4	0	8	15	Montreal Canadiens
1968-69	Toronto	4	0	0	24	5	
	Canadiens	2	4	0	16	15	Montreal Canadiens
1969-70	Rangers	4	2	0	25	16	
	Chicago	4	0	0	20	10	
	St. Louis	4	0	0	20	7	BOSTON BRUINS
1970-71	Canadiens	3	4	0	26	28	Montreal Canadiens
1971-72	Toronto	4	1	0	18	10	
	St. Louis	4	0	0	28	8	
	Rangers	4	2	0	18	16	BOSTON BRUINS
1972-73	Rangers	1	4	0	11	22	Montreal Canadiens
1973-74	Toronto	4	0	0	17	19	
	Chicago	4	2	0	28	20	
	Philadelphia	2	4	0	13	15	Philadelphia Flyers
1974-75	Chicago	1	2	0	15	12	Philadelphia Flyers
Totals		121	127	6	688	685	

HOME-ROAD RECORD

	In Boston					On Road					
				Goals					**Goals**		
Season	Won	Lost	Tied	For	Agst.	Won	Lost	Tied	For	Agst.	Coach
1924-25	3	12	0	22	57	3	12	0	27	62	A. Ross
1925-26	10	7	1	40	34	7	8	3	52	51	A. Ross
1926-27	15	7	0	61	38	6	13	3	36	51	A. Ross
1927-28	13	4	5	44	28	7	9	6	33	42	A. Ross
1928-29	16	6	1	54	25	10	7	4	35	27	A. Ross
1929-30	23	1	0	104	45	15	4	1	75	53	A. Ross
1930-31	17	1	5	83	39	11	9	1	60	51	A. Ross
1931-32	11	10	3	80	64	4	11	9	42	53	A. Ross
1932-33	20	2	3	87	39	5	13	5	37	49	A. Ross
1933-34	11	11	2	53	51	7	14	3	58	79	A. Ross
1934-35	17	7	0	75	56	9	9	6	54	56	F. Patrick
1935-36	15	8	1	47	32	7	12	5	45	51	F. Patrick
1936-37	9	11	4	61	63	14	7	3	59	47	A. Ross
1937-38	18	3	3	76	36	12	8	4	66	53	A. Ross
1938-39	20	2	2	91	39	16	8	0	65	37	A. Ross
1939-40	20	3	1	110	42	11	9	4	60	56	R. Weiland
1940-41	15	4	5	92	63	12	4	8	76	39	R. Weiland
1941-42	17	4	3	97	48	8	13	3	63	70	A. Ross
1942-43	17	3	5	121	85	7	14	4	74	91	A. Clapper
1943-44	15	8	2	120	112	4	18	3	103	156	A. Clapper
1944-45	11	12	2	100	93	5	18	2	79	126	A. Clapper
1945-46	16	5	4	97	68	8	13	4	70	88	A. Clapper
1946-47	18	7	5	112	74	8	16	6	78	101	A. Clapper
1947-48	12	8	10	85	80	11	16	3	82	88	A. Clapper
1948-49	18	10	2	102	69	11	13	6	76	94	A. Clapper
1949-50	15	12	8	112	98	7	20	8	86	130	G. Boucher
1950-51	13	12	10	102	85	9	18	8	76	112	L. Patrick
1951-52	15	12	8	84	77	10	17	8	78	99	L. Patrick
1952-53	19	10	6	98	76	9	19	7	54	96	L. Patrick
1953-54	22	8	5	99	68	10	20	5	78	113	L. Patrick
1954-55	16	10	9	109	83	7	16	12	60	105	L. Patrick—
											M. Schmidt
1955-56	14	14	7	82	84	9	20	6	65	101	M. Schmidt
1956-57	20	9	6	113	81	14	15	6	82	93	M. Schmidt
1957-58	15	14	6	108	99	12	14	9	91	95	M. Schmidt
1958-59	21	11	3	108	97	11	18	6	97	118	M. Schmidt
1959-60	21	11	3	135	102	7	23	5	85	139	M. Schmidt
1960-61	13	16	5	105	114	2	26	8	71	140	M. Schmidt
1961-62	9	22	4	91	139	6	25	4	86	167	P. Watson
1962-63	7	18	10	103	130	7	21	7	95	151	P. Watson—
											M. Schmidt
1963-64	13	15	7	98	101	5	25	5	72	111	M. Schmidt
1964-65	12	17	6	89	106	9	26	0	77	147	M. Schmidt
1965-66	15	17	3	99	119	6	26	3	75	156	M. Schmidt
1966-67	10	21	4	105	129	7	22	6	77	124	H. Sinden
1967-68	22	9	6	150	98	15	18	4	109	117	H. Sinden
1968-69	29	3	6	182	98	13	15	10	121	123	H. Sinden
1969-70	27	3	8	161	86	13	14	11	116	130	H. Sinden
1970-71	33	4	2	214	101	24	10	5	185	166	T. Johnson
1971-72	28	4	7	177	84	26	9	4	153	120	T. Johnson
1972-73	27	10	2	185	111	24	12	3	145	124	T. Johnson
											B. Guidolin
1973-74	33	4	2	193	95	19	13	7	156	126	B. Guidolin
1974-75	29	5	6	211	131	11	21	8	134	144	D. Cherry

INDIVIDUAL RECORDS

Most seasons—20—Aubrey "Dit" Clapper (1927-28 thru 1946-47)

Most games—1257—John Bucyk (18 seasons)

Most games, including playoffs—1349—John Bucyk

Most goals—484—John Bucyk (18 seasons)

Most assists—711—John Bucyk (18 seasons)

Most points—1195—John Bucyk (18 seasons)

Most goals, including playoffs—522—John Bucyk

Most assists, including playoffs—763—John Bucyk

Most points, including playoffs—1285—John Bucyk

Most shutouts by a goal tender—35—Frank Brimsek (9 seasons)

Most games scoring three or more goals—22—Phil Esposito

Most 20-or-more-goal seasons—14—John Bucyk

Most consecutive 20-or-more-goal seasons—8—Phil Esposito (1967-68—1974-75); John Bucyk (1967-68—1974-75)

Most 30-or-more-goal seasons—8—Phil Esposito

Most consecutive 30-or-more-goal seasons—8—Phil Esposito (1967-68—1974-75)

* Most 40-goal seasons—7—Phil Esposito

Most consecutive 40-goal seasons—7—Phil Esposito (1968-69—1974-75)

Most 50-goal seasons—5—Phil Esposito

* Most consecutive 50-goal seasons—5—Phil Esposito (1970-71—1974-75)

* Most 60-goal seasons—4—Phil Esposito

* Most consecutive 60-goal seasons—2—Phil Esposito (1970-71—1971-72; 1973-74—1974-75)

* Most 100-or-more-point seasons—6—Phil Esposito, Bobby Orr

* Most consecutive 100-or-more-point seasons—6—Bobby Orr (1969-70—1974-75)

* Most goals, one season—76—Phil Esposito (1970-71, 78 games)

* Most assists, one season—102—Bobby Orr (1970-71, 78 games)

* Most points one season—152—Phil Esposito (1970-71, 78 games)

* Most goals, one season, including playoffs—79—Phil Esposito (1970-71)

* Most assists, one season, including playoffs—109—Bobby Orr (1970-71)

* Most points, one season, including playoffs—162—Phil Esposito (1970-71)

* Most goals, one season, by a defense man—46—Bobby Orr (1974-75, 80 games)

* Most goals, one season, by a center—76—Phil Esposito (1970-71, 78 games); 43—Cooney Weiland (1929-30, 44 games)

Most goals, one season, by a right wing—50—Ken Hodge (1973-74, 78 games)

Most goals, one season, by a left wing—51—John Bucyk (1970-71, 78 games); 36—Herb Cain (1943-44, 50 games)

Most goals, one season, by a rookie—26—Roy Conacher (1938-39)

* Most assists, one season, by a defense man—102—Bobby Orr (1970-71, 78 games)

* Most assists, one season, by a center—77—Phil Esposito (1968-69, 1973-74)

* Most assists, one season, by a right wing—62—Ken Hodge (1970-71, 78 games)

* Most assists, one season, by a left wing—65—John Bucyk (1970-71, 78 games)

Most assists, one season, by a rookie—28—Bobby Orr (1966-67)

* Most assists, one season, by a goal tender—4—Ed Johnston (1971-72)

* Most points, one season, by a defense man—139—Bobby Orr (1970-71, 78 games)

* Most points, one season, by a center—152—Phil Esposito (1970-71, 78 games); 73—Cooney Weiland (1929-30, 44 games)

* Most points, one season, by a right wing—105—Ken Hodge (1970-71, 1973-74, 78 games)

* Most points, one season, by a left wing—116—John Bucyk (1970-71, 78 games)

Most points, one season, by a rookie—50—Gregg Sheppard (24g, 26a)

* Most power-play goals, one season—26—Phil Esposito (1971-72, 78 games)

Most short-handed goals, one season—7—Jerry Toppazzini (1957-58, 70 games), Ed Westfall (1970-71, 78 games)

Most goals by a line, one season—140—Center Phil Esposito, 76; Right Wing Ken Hodge, 43; Left Wing Wayne Cashman, 21.

Most points by a line, one season—336—Center Phil Esposito, 152; Right Wing Ken Hodge, 105; Left Wing Wayne Cashman, 79.

* Most shots on goal, one season—550—Phil Esposito (1970-71, 78 games)

Most penalty minutes, one season—165—Eddie Shore (1927-28, 44 games)

Most penalty minutes, one season, by a defense man—165—Eddie Shore (1927-28, 44 games)

Most shutouts, one season—15—Hal Winkler (1927-28, 44 games)

Most consecutive scoreless minutes by a goal tender—231.54—Frank Brimsek (1938-39)

Most consecutive shutouts by a goal tender—3—Hal Winkler (1927-28), Tiny Thompson (1935-36), Frank Brimsek (1938-39, twice)

* Longest consecutive winning streak by a goal tender—14—Ross Brooks (1973-74)

Longest consecutive goal-scoring streak—9—Phil Esposito (1970-71, 14g)

Most goals, one game—4—Cooney Weiland (vs. Pittsburgh, Feb. 25, 1930); Roy Conacher (vs. Chicago, Feb. 21, 1939); Herb Cain (vs. Toronto, Jan. 12, 1940); Bill Cowley (vs. New York, Mar. 4, 1944); Herb Cain (vs. Toronto, Jan. 16, 1945); Bill Cowley (vs. New York, Jan. 21, 1945); Woody Dumart (vs. Chicago, Mar., 1951); Pit Martin (vs. Chicago, Jan. 27, 1966); Phil Esposito (vs. Montreal, Oct. 15, 1967); Phil Esposito (vs. Buffalo, Jan. 14, 1973); John Bucyk (vs. New York Islanders, Jan. 18, 1973); Phil Esposito (vs. New York Rangers, Mar. 28, 1973); Chris Oddleifson (vs. California, Dec. 30, 1973); John Bucyk (vs. New York Islanders, Jan. 5, 1974)

Most assists, one game—6—Ken Hodge (Feb. 9, 1971, vs. New York), Bobby Orr (Jan. 1, 1973, vs. Vancouver)

Most points, one game—7—Bobby Orr (3g, 4a vs. New York Rangers, Nov. 15, 1973)

Most goals, one game, by a defense man—3—Bobby Orr (4 times)

Most assists, one game, by a defense man—6—Bobby Orr

Most goals, one game, by a rookie—4—Chris Oddleifson, Dec. 30, 1973

Most assists, one game, by a rookie—4—Derek Sanderson (vs. Chicago, Jan. 21, 1968)

Most penalties, one game—7—Ted Green (at New York, Dec. 26, 1965—3 minors, 2 majors, 2 10-minute misconducts)

Most penalty minutes, one game—37—Don Awrey (vs. Montreal— 1 minor, 3 majors, 1 10-minute misconduct, 1 game misconduct)

* Most game-winning goals—16—Phil Esposito (1970-71 and 1971-72, 78 games)

* Most goal tenders a season—5—1943-44 (Bert Gardiner, Rev. George Abbott, Maurice Courteau, Jimmy Franks, Benny Grant)
1957-58 (Don Simmons, Harry Lumley, Al Millar, Claude Evans, Ross "Lefty" Wilson)
1965-66 (Gerry Cheevers, Ed Johnston, Jack Norris, Bernie Parent, Bobby Ring)

* Most power-play goals a game by a defense man—3—Bobby Orr (Nov. 15, 1973, vs. New York Rangers)

* —League Record

219

TEAM RECORDS

* Most points a season—121 (1970-71, 78 games)
* Most games won, season—57 (1970-71, 78 games)
Most games lost, season—47 (1961-62, 70 games)
Most games tied, season—21 (1954-55, 70 games)
Fewest points, season—12 (1924-25, 30 games)
        38 (1961-62, 70 games)
Fewest games won, season— 6 (1924-25, 30 games)
        14 (1962-63, 70 games)
Fewest games lost, season— 5 (1929-30, 44 games)
        13 (1971-72, 78 games)
* Fewest games tied, season—0 (1924-25, 30 games)
        1 (1929-30, 44 games)
* Most goals scored, season—399 (1970-71, 78 games)
* Most assists, season—697 (1970-71, 78 games)
* Most scoring points, season—1096 (1970-71, 78 games)
Most points, one team, one period—22, 2nd period vs. Toronto—
    8 goals, 14 assists, March 16, 1969
Most goals allowed, season—306 (1961-62, 70 games)
Fewest goals scored, season— 49 (1924-25, 30 games)
        147 (1955-56, 70 games)
Fewest goals allowed, season—52 (1928-29, 44 games)
Most goals scored, game—14 (14-3 vs. New York Rangers, Jan. 21,
    1945)
Most goals scored, game, at home—14 (14-3 vs. New York Rangers,
    Jan. 21, 1945)
Most goals scored, game, on road—13 (at New York, Jan. 2, 1944)
Most goals allowed, game—13 (4-13 at Montreal, Nov. 21, 1943)
Most goals allowed, game, at home—10 (2-10 vs. Ottawa, Dec. 15,
    1924; 1-10 vs. Toronto, Dec. 22, 1924; 1-10 vs. Detroit, Dec. 11,
    1952; 1-10 vs. Chicago, Dec. 4, 1965; 2-10 vs. Chicago, Dec. 8,
    1966)
Most goals allowed, game, on road—13 (4-13 at Montreal, Nov. 21,
    1943)
Most goals, both teams—19 (10-9 vs. New York, March 4, 1944; 9-10
    at Detroit, March 16, 1944)
* Fastest four goals, one team—Bruins vs. New York Rangers, Jan. 21,
    1945—1 min., 20 sec. (Bill Thoms, Frank Mario twice, Ken Smith)—
    Boston won 14-3
* Fastest three goals, one team—3rd pd. vs. Vancouver, Feb. 25, 1971—
    20 sec. (John Bucyk, Ed Westfall, Ted Green)—Boston won 8-3
* Fastest two goals from start of game, one team—37 sec., Jan. 31, 1943,
    at New York (Buzz Boll, 14 sec.; Bill Cowley, 37 sec.)—Bruins
    won 7-2
* Most consecutive games won—14 (Dec. 3—Jan. 12, 1924-25)
* Most consecutive games without losing—23 (Dec. 22, 1940—Feb. 5,
    1941; won 15, tied 8)
Most consecutive games lost—11 (Dec. 3, 1924—Jan. 5, 1925)
Most consecutive games without win—20 (Jan. 28—March 11, 1962)
Most consecutive games tied—4 (1931-32, 1940-41, 1953-54, 1960-61)
* Most consecutive games won at home—22 (1929-30)
* Most home victories, season—33 (1970-71)
Most consecutive games lost at home, season—11 (1924-25)

* —League Record

Most consecutive games tied, season, at home—3 (1940-41, 1951-52,
    1953-54, 1960-61)
Most consecutive games won on road, season—8 (1971-72)
* Most road victories, season—26 (1971-72, 78 games)
Most consecutive games lost on road, season—12 (1965-66)
Most consecutive games without losing at home—27 (Nov. 22, 1970—
    March 20, 1971; won 26, tied 1)
* Most consecutive games without losing on road, season—15 (Dec. 22,
    1940—March 16, 1941; won 9, tied 6)
Total shutouts—275 (173 at home, 102 on road)
Total shutouts against—234 (83 at home, 151 on road)
Most shutouts for, season—15 (1927-28)
Most shutouts against, season—11 (1928-29, 1955-56)
Fewest shutouts for, season—0 (1944-45)
Fewest shutouts against, season—0 (1929-30)
Most consecutive shutouts for, season—3 (1927-28, 1936-36, 1938-39
    twice)
Most consecutive shutouts against, season—3 (1928-29)
Most consecutive games without being shutout, overlapping seasons—
    112 (Jan. 21, 1972, to April 7, 1974)
Most consecutive games without scoring shutout, overlapping sea-
    sons—71 (Feb. 10, 1942, to Nov. 21, 1945)
Most consecutive shutouts scored at home—3 (1926-27, 1927-28, 1928-
    29, 1932-33, 1953-54)
Most consecutive shutouts scored on road—4 (1938-39)
Biggest shutout for—11-0 (at Toronto, Jan. 18, 1964)
Biggest shutout against—0-8 (at Detroit, Feb. 7, 1937; at Toronto, Mar.
    25, 1950; at Chicago, Feb. 25, 1962; at Montreal, Mar. 7, 1964)
* Most power-play goals, season—81 (1969-70)
* Most power-play goals against, season—80 (1969-70)
* Most short-handed goals for, season—25 (Ed Westfall, 7; Don Marcotte,
    6; Derek Sanderson, 6; Bobby Orr, 3; Dallas Smith, 2; Phil Esposito,
    1—1970-71)
* Most 20-goal-or-more scorers, 1 season—10 (Phil Esposito, Bobby Orr,
    John Bucyk, Ken Hodge, Wayne Cashman, John McKenzie, Fred
    Stanfield, Derek Sanderson, Ed Westfall, Wayne Carleton—1970-71)
* Most 30-goal-or-more scorers, 1 season—5 (Phil Esposito, John Bucyk,
    Ken Hodge, Bobby Orr, John McKenzie—1970-71) (Phil Esposito,
    Bobby Orr, Ken Hodge, John Bucyk, Wayne Cashman—1973-74)
* Most 40-goal-or-more scorers, 1 season—3 (Phil Esposito, John Bucyk,
    Ken Hodge—1970-71)
* Most 50-goal-or-more scorers, 1 season—2 (Phil Esposito, John Bucyk—
    1970-71; Phil Esposito, Ken Hodge—1973-74)
* Most 100-point-or-more scorers, 1 season—4 (Phil Esposito, 152; Bobby
    Orr, 139; John Bucyk, 116; Ken Hodge, 105—1970-71)
* First four scorers in individual scoring race—(Phil Esposito, Bobby Orr,
    John Bucyk, Ken Hodge—1970-71) (Phil Esposito, Bobby Orr, Ken
    Hodge, Wayne Cashman—1973-74)
* Most three-goal games, 1 season—14 (Phil Esposito, 7; John Bucyk, 3;
    John McKenzie, 2; Ed Westfall, 1; Wayne Carleton, 1—1970-71)
Most penalty minutes, 1 season—1,297 (1968-69)

* —League Record

LISTING OF ALL BRUINS PLAYERS

George Abbott	1943-44	Adam Brown	1951-52
John Adams	1972-73	Wayne Brown	1953-54
Gary Aldcorn	1960-61	Gordie Bruce	1940-41—1941-42;
Earl Anderson	1974-75		1945-46
John Arbour	1965-66—1967-68	Ron Buchanan	1966-67
Bob Armstrong	1950-51—1961-62	Billy Burch	1932-33
Barry Ashbee	1965-66	Eddie Burke	1931-32
Steve Atkinson	1968-69	John Bucyk	1957-58—1974-75
Oscar Aubuchon	1942-43—1943-44	Charlie Burns	1959-60—1962-63
Don Awrey	1963-64—1972-73	Gordon Byers	1949-50
Pete Babando	1947-48—1948-49	Jack Caffery	1956-57—1957-58
Garnet Bailey	1968-69—1972-73	Charles Cahill	1925-26
Murray Balfour	1964-65	Herb Cain	1939-40—1945-46
Stan Baluik	1959-60	Norm Calladine	1942-43—1944-45
Eddie Barry	1946-47	Wayne Carleton	1969-70—1970-71
Marty Barry	1929-30—1934-35	George Carroll	1925-26
Ray Barry	1951-52	Bill Carson	1928-29—1929-30
Jimmy Bartlett	1960-61	Billy Carter	1960-61
Bobby Bauer	1936-37—1941-42;	Wayne Cashman	1964-65; 1967-68—
	1945-46—1946-47; 1951-52		1974-75
Red Beattie	1930-31; 1932-33—	Joe Carveth	1946-47—1947-48
	1936-37	Ed Chadwick	1961-62
Bob Beckett	1956-57—1957-58—	Murph Chamberlain	1942-43
	1963-64	Art Chapman	1930-31—1933-34
Harvey Bennett	1944-45	Gerry Cheevers	1965-66—1971-72
Bobby Benson	1924-25	Dick Cherry	1956-57
Fred Bergdinon	1925-26	Don Cherry	1954-55
Sam Bettio	1949-50	Real Chevrefils	1951-52—1958-59
Nick Beverley	1966-67; 1969-70;	Art Chisholm	1960-61
	1971-72—1973-74	Jack Church	1945-46
Paul Bibeault	1945-46	Aubrey "Dit" Clapper	1927-28—1946-47
Jack Bionda	1956-57—1958-59	Nobby Clark	1927-28
Dick Bittner	1949-50	Sprague Cleghorn	1925-26—1927-28
Don Blackburn	1962-63	Les Colvin	1948-49
Gus Bodnar	1953-54—1954-55	Roy Conacher	1938-39—1941-42;
Leo Boivin	1954-55—1965-66		1945-46
Ivan Boldirev	1970-71—1971-72	Wayne Connelly	1961-62—1963-64;
Frank "Buzz" Boll	1942-43—1943-44		1966-67
Marcel Bonin	1955-56	Harry Connor	1927-28—1929-30
Carl "Buddy" Boone	1956-57—1957-58	Alex Cook	1931-32
Billy Boucher	1926-27	Fred "Bun" Cook	1936-37
Irwin "Yank" Boyd	1931-32—	Lloyd Cook	1924-25
	1942-43—1943-44	Carson Cooper	1924-25—1926-27
Spider Brackenborough	1925-26	Norm Corcoran	1949-50—1952-53—
Barton Bradley	1949-50		1954-55
Tom Brennan	1943-44—1944-45	Murray Costello	1954-55—1955-56
Archie Briden	1926-27	Maurice Courteau	1943-44
Frank Brimsek	1938-39—1942-43;	Billy Coutu	1926-27
	1945-46—1948-49	Bill Cowley	1935-36—1946-47
Ken Broderick	1973-74—1974-75	John Crawford	1938-39—1949-50
Ross Brooks	1972-73—1974-75	Dave Creighton	1948-49—1953-54

Terry Crisp	1965-66	Barry Gibbs	1967-68—1968-69
Wilf Cude	1931-32	Doug Gibson	1973-74
Bill Cupolo	1944-45	Gilles Gilbert	1973-74—1974-75
		Jeannot Gilbert	1962-63—1964-65
Nick Damore	1941-42	Andre Gill	1967-68
Hal Darragh	1930-31	Art Giroux	1934-35
Pinkie Davis	1933-34—1935-36	Paul Gladu	1944-45
Lorne Davis	1955-56—1959-60	Warren Godfrey	1952-53—1954-55—
Murray Davison	1965-66		1962-63
Norm Defelice	1956-57	Bill Goldsworthy	1964-65—1966-67
Armand "Dutch" Delmonte	1942-43—1943-44	Roy Goldsworthy	1936-37—1937-38
Ab DeMarco	1942-43—1943-44	Fred Gordon	1927-28
Cy Denneny	1928-29	Bob Gracie	1933-34
Gerry Desrosiers	1941-42	Ted Graham	1935-36
Bob Dillabough	1965-66—1966-67	Benny Grant	1943-44
Gary Doak	1965-66—1969-70; 1973-74—1974-75	Terry Gray	1961-62
Gary Dornhoefer	1963-64—1965-66	Redvers "Red" Green	1928-29
Lorne Duguid	1935-36—1936-37	Ted Green	1960-61—1968-69; 1970-71—1971-72
Woody Dumart	1936-37—1941-42; 1945-46—1953-54	Lloyd Gronsdahl	1941-42
		Lloyd Gross	1933-34
Darryl Edestrand	1973-74—1974-75	Don Grosso	1946-47
Pat Egan	1943-44—1948-49	Bob Gryp	1973-74
Gerry Ehman	1957-58	Armand "Bep" Guidolin	1942-43—1943-44; 1945-46—1946-47
Leighton "Hap" Emms	1934-35		
Aut Erickson	1959-60—1960-61		
Grant Erickson	1968-69	Robert "Red" Hamill	1937-38—1941-42
Phil Esposito	1967-68—1974-75	Walter "Happy" Harnott	1933-34
Claude Evans	1957-58	Leland "Hago" Harrington	1925-26; 1927-28
Bill Ezinicki	1951-52	Fred Harris	1924-25
Lorne Ferguson	1949-50—1950-51; 1954-55—1955-56	Smokey Harris	1930-31
		Ed Harrison	1947-48—1950-51
Guyle Fielder	1953-54	Jim Harrison	1968-69—1969-70
Marcel Fillion	1944-45	Chris Hayes	1971-72
Dunc Fisher	1950-51—1952-53	Paul Haynes	1934-35
Ferny Flaman	1945-46—1950-51; 1954-55—1960-61	Don Head	1961-62
		Curley Headley	1924-25
Reg Fleming	1964-65—1965-66	Andy Hebenton	1963-64
David Forbes	1973-74—1974-75	Lionel Heinrich	1955-56
Harry "Yip" Foster	1931-32	Murray Henderson	1944-45—1951-52
Hec Fowler	1924-25	John Henderson	1954-55—1955-56
Jim Franks	1943-44	Gordon "Red" Henry	1948-49—1950-51—1952-53
Frank Fredrickson	1926-27—1928-29		
		Jim Henry	1951-52—1954-55
Art Gagne	1929-30	Phil Hergesheimer	1941-42
Pierre Gagne	1959-60	Jimmy Herberts	1924-25—1927-28
Johnny Gagnon	1934-35	Obs Heximer	1932-33
Norman "Dutch" Gainor	1927-28—1930-31	Wayne Hicks	1962-63
Percy "Perk" Galbraith	1926-27—1933-34	Mel Hill	1937-38—1940-41
Don Gallinger	1941-42—1943-44; 1945-46—1947-48	Wilbert "Dutch" Hiller	1941-42—1942-43
		Floyd Hillman	1956-57
Bruce Gamble	1960-61—1961-62	Larry Hillman	1957-58—1959-60
Bert Gardiner	1943-44	Lionel Hitchman	1924-25—1933-34
Cal Gardner	1953-54—1956-57	Ken Hodge	1967-68—1974-75
Ray Gariepy	1953-54	Ted Hodgson	1966-67
Armand Gaudreault	1944-45	Bill "Flash" Hollett	1935-36—1943-44
Jean Gauthier	1968-69	Pete Horeck	1949-50
Jack Gelineau	1948-49—1950-51	Bronco Horvath	1957-58—1960-61
Guy Gendron	1958-59—1960-61; 1962-63—1963-64	Paul Hurley	1968-69
		Bill Hutton	1929-30—1930-31
Ray Getliffe	1935-36—1938-39	Dave Hynes	1973-74
Gerry Geran	1925-26		
		Jack Ingram	1924-25
		Ted Irvine	1963-64

Art Jackson	1937-38; 1939-40—1944-45
Harvey Jackson	1941-42—1943-44
Percy Jackson	1931-32
Stan Jackson	1924-25—1925-26
Bill Jennings	1944-45
Roger Jenkins	1935-36
Frank Jerwa	1931-32—1932-33
Joe Jerwa	1933-34—1935-36
Norm Johnson	1957-58—1958-59
Tom Johnson	1963-64—1964-65
Ed Johnston	1962-63—1972-73
Ron Jones	1970-71—1972-73
Joe Junkin	1968-69
Max Kaminsky	1934-35—1935-36
Duke Keats	1926-27
Forbes Kennedy	1962-63—1965-66
Lloyd Klein	1928-29—1931-32
Joe Klukay	1952-53—1954-55
Bill Knibbs	1964-65
Russ Kopak	1943-44
Steve Kraftcheck	1950-51
Phil "Skip" Krake	1963-64—1965-66; 1967-68
Ed Kryzanowski	1948-49—1951-52
Arnie Kullman	1947-48—1949-50
Orland Kurtenbach	1961-62—1963-64—1964-65
Gus Kyle	1951-52
Leo LaBine	1951-52—1960-61
Guy Labrie	1943-44
Joe Lamb	1932-33—1933-34
Myles Lane	1933-34
Al Langlois	1965-66
Bonner LaRose	1925-26
Martin Lauder	1927-28
Hal Laycoe	1950-51—1955-56
Larry Leach	1958-59—1959-60; 1961-62
Reg Leach	1970-71—1971-72
Richie Leduc	1972-73—1973-74
Bob Leiter	1962-63—1964-65—1968-69
Bill Lesuk	1968-69—1969-70
Pete Leswick	1944-45
Holes Lockhart	1924-25—1925-26
Ross Lonsberry	1966-67—1968-69
Jim Lorentz	1968-69—1969-70
Ross Lowe	1949-50—1950-51
Harry Lumley	1957-58—1959-60
Pentti Lund	1946-47; 1951-52—1952-53
Vic Lynn	1950-51—1951-52
Peaches Lyons	1930-31
Parker MacDonald	1965-66
Mickey Mackay	1928-29—1929-30
Fleming Mackell	1951-52—1959-60
Phil Maloney	1949-50—1950-51
Ray Manson	1947-48
Sylvio Mantha	1936-37
Don Marcotte	1965-66; 1968-69—1971-72; 1973-74—1974-75

Frank Mario	1941-42—1944-45
Gil Marotte	1965-66—1966-67
Mark Marquess	1946-47
Clare Martin	1941-42; 1946-47—1947-48
Frank Martin	1952-53—1953-54
Hubert "Pit" Martin	1965-66—1966-67
Joe Matte	1925-26
Wayne Maxner	1964-65—1965-66
Norm McAtee	1946-47
Tom McCarthy	1960-61
Bob McCord	1963-64—1964-65
Ab McDonald	1964-65
Jack McGill	1941-42; 1944-45—1946-47
Bert McInenly	1933-34—1934-35
Jack McIntyre	1949-50—1952-53
Walt McKechnie	1974-75
Don McKenney	1954-55—1962-63
John McKenzie	1965-66—1971-72
Mike McMahon, Sr.	1945-46
Pat McReavy	1939-40—1941-42
Harry Meeking	1926-27
Dick Meissner	1959-60—1961-62
Al Millar	1957-58
Herb Mitchell	1924-25—1925-26
Doug Mohns	1953-54—1963-64
Bernie Morris	1924-25
Jim Morrison	1951-52—1958-59
Alex Motter	1935-36—1937-38
Ron Murphy	1965-66—1969-70
Al Nicholson	1955-56—1956-57
Jack Norris	1964-65—1965-66
Hank Nowak	1974-75
Ellard O'Brien	1965-66
Chris Oddleifson	1972-73—1973-74
Fred O'Donnell	1972-73
Harry Oliver	1926-27—1933-34
Murray Oliver	1960-61—1966-67
Peggy O'Neil	1933-34—1936-37
Willie O'Ree	1957-58—1960-61
Terry O'Reilly	1971-72—1974-75
Bobby Orr	1966-67—1974-75
Gerry Ouellette	1960-61
George Owen	1928-29—1932-33
Al Pallazzari	1943-44
Ed Panagabko	1955-56—1956-57
Bernie Parent	1965-66—1966-67
Jean Paul Parise	1965-66—1966-67
George Patterson	1933-34
John Peirson	1946-47—1953-54; 1955-56—1957-58
Cliff Pennington	1961-62—1962-63
Bob Perreault	1962-63
Garry Peters	1971-72
Jimmy Peters	1947-48—1948-49
Eric Pettinger	1928-29
Gordon Pettinger	1937-38—1939-40
Harry Pidhirny	1957-58
Jacques Plante	1972-73
Norman "Bud" Poile	1949-50
Dan Poliziani	1958-59

Paul Popiel	1965-66
Jack Portland	1934-35; 1936-37— 1939-40
Jack Pratt	1930-31—1931-32
Walter "Babe" Pratt	1946-47
Dean Prentice	1962-63—1965-66
Andre Pronovost	1960-61—1962-63
Claude Pronovost	1955-56
Jean Pusie	1934-35
Bill Quackenbush	1949-50—1955-56
Max Quackenbush	1950-51
John Quilty	1947-48
George Ranieri	1956-57
Matt Ravlich	1962-63—1972-73
Terry Reardon	1939-40—1940-41; 1945-46—1946-47
Gordon Redahl	1958-59
George Redding	1924-25—1925-26
Larry Regan	1956-57—1958-59
Earl Reibel	1958-59
Ed Reigle	1950-51
Jack Riley	1935-36
Bobby Ring	1965-66
Vic Ripley	1932-33—1933-34
Alan Rittinger	1943-44
Wayne Rivers	1963-64—1966-67
Doug Roberts	1971-72—1973-74
Morris Roberts	1925-26
Eddie Rodden	1928-29
Dale Rolfe	1959-60
Paul Ronty	1947-48—1949-50
Bobby Rowe	1924-25
Gino Rozzini	1944-45
Paul Runge	1931-32—1935-36
Derek Sanderson	1965-66—1973-74
Ed Sandford	1947-48—1954-55
Charlie Sands	1934-35—1938-39
Glen Sather	1966-67—1968-69
Gordon Savage	1934-35
Andre Savard	1973-74—1974-75
Terry Sawchuk	1955-56—1956-57
Charlie Scherza	1943-44
Bob Schmautz	1973-74—1974-75
Clarence Schmidt	1943-44
John Schmidt	1942-43
Joseph Schmidt	1943-44
Milt Schmidt	1936-37—1941-42; 1946-47—1954-55
Werner Schnarr	1924-25—1925-26
Dan Schock	1969-70—1970-71
Ron Schock	1963-64—1966-67
Ed Shack	1967-68—1968-69
Normie Shay	1924-25—1925-26
Jerry Shannon	1934-35—1935-36
John Shepherd	1933-34
Gregg Sheppard	1972-73—1974-75
Jack Shewchuk	1938-39; 1942-43— 1944-45
Bill Shill	1942-43; 1945-46—1946-47
Jack Shill	1934-35
Allan Shields	1936-37
Eddie Shore	1926-27—1939-40
Albert "Babe" Siebert	1933-34—1935-36

Al Simmons	1973-74
Don Simmons	1956-57—1960-61
Al Sims	1973-74—1974-75
Alfie Skinner	1924-25
Don Smillie	1933-34
Alex Smith	1932-33—1933-34
Dallas Smith	1959-60—1961-62; 1965-66—1974-75
Des Smith	1939-40—1941-42
Floyd Smith	1954-55—1956-57
Ken Smith	1944-45—1950-51
Reginald "Hooley" Smith	1936-37
Rick Smith	1968-69—1971-72
Spunk Sparrow	1924-25
Bill Speer	1969-70—1970-71
Irvin Spencer	1962-63
Frank Spring	1969-70—1970-71
Fred Stanfield	1967-68—1971-72
Allan Stanley	1956-57—1957-58
Pat Stapleton	1961-62
Vic Stasiuk	1955-56—1960-61
Phil Stevens	1925-26
Bob Stewart	1971-72
Charles "Doc" Stewart	1924-25—1926-27
Nels Stewart	1932-33—1934-35; 1936-37
Ron Stewart	1965-66—1966-67
Red Stuart	1924-25—1926-27
George "Red" Sullivan	1949-50—1952-53
Billy Taylor	1947-48
Bobby Taylor	1929-30
Allan "Skip" Teal	1954-55
Orval Tessier	1955-56—1960-61
Cecil "Tiny" Thompson	1928-29—1938-39
Cliff Thompson	1941-42—1948-49
Bill Thoms	1944-45
Jerry Toppazzini	1952-53—1953-54; 1955-56—1963-64
Zellio Toppazzini	1948-49—1949-50
George Tuohey	1931-32
Geordon Turlik	1959-60
Carol Vadnais	1971-72—1974-75
Mike Walton	1970-71—1972-73
Don Ward	1959-60
Grant Warwick	1947-48—1948-49
Joe Watson	1964-65—1966-67
Tom Webster	1968-69—1969-70
Ralph "Cooney" Weiland	1928-29— 1931-32; 1935-36—1938-39
Ed Westfall	1961-62—1971-72
Archie Wilcox	1933-34
Jack Wilkenson	1943-44
Barry Wilkins	1966-67—1968-69
Burr Williams	1934-35
Tom Williams	1961-62—1968-69
Gordie Wilson	1954-55
Ross "Lefty" Wilson	1957-58
Wally Wilson	1947-48
Hal Winkler	1926-27—1927-28
Ed Wiseman	1939-40—1941-42
Bob Woytowich	1964-65—1966-67
Ken Yackel	1958-59